Raku Fundamentals

A Primer with Examples, Projects, and Case Studies

Second Edition

Moritz Lenz
Foreword by Larry Wall, creator of Raku

Apress®

Raku Fundamentals: A Primer with Examples, Projects, and Case Studies

Moritz Lenz
Fürth, Bayern, Germany

ISBN-13 (pbk): 978-1-4842-6108-8   ISBN-13 (electronic): 978-1-4842-6109-5
https://doi.org/10.1007/978-1-4842-6109-5

Managing Director, Apress Media LLC: Welmoed Spahr
Acquisitions Editor: Steve Anglin
Development Editor: Matthew Moodie
Coordinating Editor: Mark Powers

Cover designed by eStudioCalamar

Cover image by Stephen Hume on Unsplash (www.unsplash.com)

Distributed to the book trade worldwide by Springer Science+Business Media, 1 New York Plaza, New York, NY 10004, U.S.A.. Phone 1-800-SPRINGER, fax (201) 348-4505, e-mail orders-ny@springer-sbm.com, or visit www.springeronline.com. Apress Media, LLC is a California LLC and the sole member (owner) is Springer Science + Business Media Finance Inc (SSBM Finance Inc). SSBM Finance Inc is a **Delaware** corporation.

For information on translations, please e-mail booktranslations@springernature.com; for reprint, paperback, or audio rights, please e-mail bookpermissions@springernature.com.

Apress titles may be purchased in bulk for academic, corporate, or promotional use. eBook versions and licenses are also available for most titles. For more information, reference our Print and eBook Bulk Sales web page at http://www.apress.com/bulk-sales.

Any source code or other supplementary material referenced by the author in this book is available to readers on GitHub via the book's product page, located at www.apress.com/9781484261088. For more detailed information, please visit http://www.apress.com/source-code.

Printed on acid-free paper

Table of Contents

About the Author

Moritz Lenz is a software engineer and architect. In the Raku community, he is well known for his contributions to the Raku programming language, the Rakudo compiler, related test suite, infrastructure, and tools. He is also a prolific Perl and Python programmer.

About the Technical Reviewer

Matt Wade is a programmer, database developer, and system administrator. He works for a large financial firm running a production support organization where he gets to solve puzzles all day long. Matt resides in Jacksonville, Florida, with his wife, Michelle, and their children, Matthew and Jonathan.

Acknowledgments

They say it takes a village to raise a child. Similar things can be said about writing a book. It is only possible through the effort of many people, often unpaid volunteers who contribute just to see the project succeed, and out of kindness of heart.

I am very grateful for the review by and feedback from Paul Cochrane, Will Coleda, Elizabeth Mattijsen, Ryan Erwin, Claudio Ramirez, Alexander Kiryuhin, Aleks-Daniel Jakimenko-Aleksejev, Matt Wade, and Massimo Nardone.

Special thanks go to Larry Wall for creating Perl and Raku, for the great foreword, and for shaping the community to be friendly, welcoming, and a second home to me.

Finally, thanks go to my parents, for kindling my love both for books and for engineering. And most importantly to my family: to Signe, my wife, for constant support and to my daughters Ida and Ronja for keeping me grounded in the real world, and bringing joy to my life.

Foreword

The reason I'm writing this (and perhaps why you're reading it) is that people just give me way too much credit. Yeah, sure, I invented Perl 30 years ago, and I coded the first five versions all by myself, pretty much. But for the last 20 years, the vast majority of the work has been done by other members of the industrious Perl[1] community, who get far too little credit. To be sure, I don't mind getting extra credit: I'm human enough to enjoy the undue adulation, and I understand how communities want—and possibly even need—to have a figurehead who represents the whole.

I will gladly take credit, however, for the idea that a computer language must have a vibrant community in order to thrive. From the beginning, that was the intent of Perl. It all comes down to linguistics: Perl was designed to work like a natural language on many levels, not just the syntactic level. In particular, every living language is symbiotic with the culture that conveys it forward into the future. More generally, natural languages are responsive to context on every level, and some of those levels are anthropological. People provide context to Perl, which in turn is designed to respond productively to that context.

This may seem simple, but it's a surprisingly tricky concept to bake into a programming language and its culture. Just look at how many computer languages fail at it. In most programming cultures, you are a slave to the computer language. Rarely, if ever, do you get the feeling that the computer language is there to work for you.

---

[1]Raku started its life as Perl 6; it was renamed after Mr. Wall has written this foreword.

We're trying to change all that. So when the Perl community, back in 2000, decided to do a major redesign of Perl 5 to clean up the cruftier bits, we not only wanted to fix things that we already knew were suboptimal, but we also wanted to do a better job of responding to cultural change, because we simply don't know what we'll want in the future. So we thought about how best to future-proof a computer language; much of the current design is about maintaining careful control of identity, mutability, dimensionality, typology, and extensibility over time, so we could isolate changes to minimize collateral damage. Other than worrying about that, my main contribution as the language designer was to unify the community's contradictory desires into a coherent whole.

All that being said, it's still all about the community: nearly all the implementation work was done by others, and most of the features that ended up in Perl 6 can be traced back through various revisions to the community's original RFCs. True, many of those original designs we deemed inadequate, but we never lost sight of the pain points those original suggestions were trying to address. As a result, even though Perl 6 ended up to be quite a different language than Perl 5, it is still essentially Perl in spirit. We now think of Perl 6 as the "younger sister" to Perl 5, and we expect the sisters will get along well in the future. You're allowed to be friends with either or both. They only squabble occasionally, as family do.

Since 2000, we've had over 800 contributors to the Perl 6 effort, one way or another. Some folks come and go, and that's fine. We welcome the occasional contributor. On the other hand, we also honor those who strove greatly but paid the price of burnout. And we deeply revere those who have already passed on, who contributed, in some cases, knowing they would never see the final result.

But then there are those who have stuck with the Perl 6 effort through thick and thin, through joy and frustration, who have patiently (or at least persistently!) risen to the challenge of building a better Perl community around the revised Perl language, and who have gladly taken on the hard work of making other people's lives easy.

One such is my friend Moritz Lenz, your author, and a much-respected member of our not-so-secret Perl 6 Cabal. Well, some days it's more like the Perl 6 Comedy Club.

While thinking about this foreword, I guessed (and Moritz confirmed) that he has a background in the performance arts. One can tell, because he seems to have a natural feel for when to blend in as part of the ensemble, when to step forward and take a solo lead, and when to step back again and let someone else come to the fore. In many ways, the Perl 6 effort has been like a jazz jam session, or like improv comedy, the kind of art where part of it is showing how cleverly we learn to work together and trade off roles on the fly.

I've had to learn some of that myself. Good leaders don't try to lead all the time. That's what bad leaders try to do. Often, a good leader is just "following out in front," sensing when the group behind wants a change of direction, and then pretending to lead the group in that direction. Moritz knows how to do that too.

Hence, this book. It's not just a reference, since you can always find such materials online. Nor is it just a cookbook. I like to think of it as an extended invitation, from a well-liked and well-informed member of our circle to people like you who might want to join in on the fun, because joy is what's fundamental to Perl. The essence of Perl is an invitation to love, and to be loved by, the Perl community. It's an invitation to be a participant of the gift economy, on both the receiving and the giving end.

Since Herr Doktor Professor Lenz is from Deutschland, I think it's appropriate to end with one of my favorite German sayings:

> Liebe ist arm und reich,
>
> Fordert und gibt zugleich.

Oder auf Englisch:

> Love is poor and rich,
>
> Taking and giving as one.

—Larry Wall, May 2017

CHAPTER 1

What Is Raku?

Raku is a programming language. It is designed to be easily learned, read, and written by humans and is inspired by natural language. It allows the beginner to write in "baby Raku," while giving the experienced programmer freedom of expression, from concise to poetic.

Raku is gradually typed. It mostly follows the paradigm of dynamically typed languages in that it accepts programs whose type safety it can't guarantee during compilation. However, unlike many dynamic languages, it accepts and enforces type constraints. Where possible, the compiler uses type annotations to make decisions at compile time that would otherwise only be possible at runtime.

Many programming paradigms have influenced Raku. It has started its life under the name "Perl 6" but has been renamed in 2019 to break the illusion that it is just another version of Perl. Besides the obvious Perl influence, it contains inspirations from Ruby, Haskell, Smalltalk, and many other languages.

You can write imperative, object-oriented, and functional programs in Raku. We will see object-oriented programming starting from Chapter 5 and a refactoring with functional approaches in Sections 10.4 and 10.5. Declarative programming is supported through features like multiple dispatch, subtyping, and the regex and grammar engine (explored in Chapter 9).

© Moritz Lenz 2020
M. Lenz, *Raku Fundamentals*, https://doi.org/10.1007/978-1-4842-6109-5_1

Most lookups in Raku are lexical, and the language avoids global state. This makes parallel and concurrent execution of programs easier, as does Raku's focus on high-level concurrency primitives. When you don't want to be limited to one CPU core, instead of thinking in terms of threads and locks, you tend to think about promises and message queues.

Raku as a language is not opinionated about whether Raku programs should be compiled or interpreted. Rakudo—the main implementation— precompiles modules on the fly and interprets scripts.

1.1 Intended Audience

To get the most out of this book, you should be interested in learning the Raku programming language and have some basic familiarity with programming.

You should know what variables, if statements, and loops are and have used some mechanisms for structuring code, be it through functions, subroutines, methods, or similar constructs. A basic understanding of object-oriented concepts such as classes, objects or instances, and methods helps but is not required.

A basic knowledge of data types such as numbers, strings (text), arrays or lists, and hashes (often also called hash maps, dictionaries, or maps) is also assumed.

If you lack this knowledge, *Think Perl 6* by Allen Downey and Laurent Rosenfeld (2017, O'Reilly Media) is good introduction.

Finally, this book is not a reference, so it assumes you are at least somewhat comfortable with looking things up, usually through the search engine of your choice or the official documentation at https://docs.raku.org/.

1.2 Perl 5: The Older Sister

Around the year 2000, Perl 5 development faced major strain from the conflicting desires to evolve and to keep backward compatibility.

Perl 6 was the valve to release this tension. All the extension proposals that required a break in backward compatibility were channeled into Perl 6, leaving it in a dreamlike state where everything was possible and nothing was fixed. It took several years of hard work to get into a more solid state.

During this time, Perl 5 also evolved, and the two languages are different enough that most Perl 5 developers don't consider Perl 6 a natural upgrade path anymore, to the point that Perl 6 does not try to obsolete Perl 5 (at least not more than it tries to obsolete any other programming language :-), and the first stable release of Perl 6 in 2015 does not indicate any lapse in support for Perl 5. The rename of Perl 6 to Raku solidified the intention of both communities to continue development of Perl and Raku separately but with collaboration through shared workshops and conferences.

Raku provides several features that have not found their way into Perl 5, mostly because they seem to require backward incompatible changes or changes too big for the fairly conservative Perl 5 developers:

- An easy-to-use, powerful object model, includes a meta-object model, built into the language.

- A rich collection of built-in types.

- A clear distinction between binary data and strings.

- A solid approach to concurrent execution with threads.

- Built-in grammars and a cleaned-up regex syntax.

On the other hand, Perl scores with maturity and an excellent track record of backward compatibility, a huge ecosystem of libraries, and predictable (and often, but not always) superior performance.

3

1.3 Library Availability

Being a relatively young language, Raku lacks the mature module ecosystem that languages such as Perl 5 and Python provide.

Nonetheless, some excellent, open source modules exist for Raku. One example is the Cro[1] HTTP framework for both client- and serverside HTTP applications, including support for HTTP/2 and reactive programming. Another is Red,[2] a cross-database object-relation mapper that makes use of Raku's extensive meta-programming capabilities to provide a smooth interface.

If you still find yourself missing libraries, interfaces exist that allow you to call into libraries written in C, Python, Perl 5, and Ruby. The Perl 5 and Python interfaces are sophisticated enough that you can write a Raku class that subclasses a class written in either language and the other way around.

So if you like a particular Python library, for example, you can simply load it into your Raku program through the `Inline::Python` module.

1.4 Why Should I Use Raku?

If you like the quick prototyping experience from dynamically typed programming languages, but you also want enough safety features to build big, reliable applications, Raku is a good fit for you. Its gradual typing allows you to write code without having a full picture of the types involved, and later introduce type constraints to guard against future misuse of your internal and external APIs.

Perl has a long history of making text processing via regular expressions (*regexes*) very easy, but more complicated regexes have acquired a reputation of being hard to read and maintain. Raku solves this

---

[1]`https://cro.services/`
[2]`https://modules.raku.org/dist/Red:cpan:FCO`

4

by putting regexes on the same level as code, allowing you to name them like subroutines and even to use object-oriented features such as class inheritance and role composition to manage code and regex reuse. The resulting grammars are very powerful and easy to read. In fact, the Rakudo compiler parses Raku source code with a grammar!

Speaking of text, Raku has amazing Unicode support. If you ask your user for a number, and they enter it with digits that don't happen to be the Arabic digits from the ASCII range, Raku still has you covered. And if you deal with graphemes that cannot be expressed as a single Unicode code point, Raku still presents it as a single character.

There are more technical benefits that I could list, but more importantly, the language is designed to be fun to use. An important aspect of that is good error messages. Have you ever been annoyed at Python for typically giving just `SyntaxError: invalid syntax` when something's wrong? This error could come from forgetting a closing parenthesis, for example. In this case, Rakudo says

```
Unable to parse expression in argument list; couldn't find
final ')'
```

which actually tells you what's wrong. But this is just the tip of the iceberg. The compiler catches common mistakes and points out possible solutions and even suggests fixes for spelling mistakes. The Raku community considers error messages that are *less than awesome*, short LTA, to be worthy of bug reports, and much effort is spent into raising the bar for error messages.

Finally, Raku gives you the freedom to express your problem domain and solution in different ways and with different programming paradigms. And if the options provided by the core language are not enough, it is designed with extensibility in mind, allowing you to introduce both new semantics for object-oriented code and new syntax.

1.5 **Summary**

Raku is a flexible programming language that offers many cool and convenient features to both beginners and experts. It offers flexibility, type checking, and powerful Unicode and text processing support.

CHAPTER 2

Running Rakudo

Before we start exploring the Raku language, you should have an environment where you can run Raku code. So you need to install Rakudo, currently the only actively developed Raku compiler. Or even better, install Rakudo Star, which is a distribution that includes Rakudo itself, a few useful modules, and a tool that can help you install more modules.

Installing Rakudo itself gives you just the compiler. It follows a monthly release cycle, so it allows you to keep up to date with the latest developments.

When you choose to install Rakudo Star, which is typically released every three months, you get a more stable base for development and some tools like a debugger and a module installer. You can use the module installer to make use of prepackaged software libraries that are included neither in Rakudo itself nor in Rakudo Star. Some examples in this book will require some modules from the ecosystem, so you should install Rakudo in a way that lets you use zef, the module installer.

The following sections discuss a few options for installing Rakudo Star. Choose whatever works for you.

The examples in this book use Rakudo 2020.01 and should work with this or any newer version of Rakudo, as long as it supports Raku version 6.d.

© Moritz Lenz 2020

M. Lenz, *Raku Fundamentals*, https://doi.org/10.1007/978-1-4842-6109-5_2

Note   The examples and source code used in this book can be accessed via the Download Source Code button at https://www.apress.com/ 9781484261088. You can also obtain the source code through git with this command: git clone https://github.com/apress/ raku-fundamentals.git

---

2.1 Installers

You can download installers from https://rakudo.org/star for Mac OS (.dmg) and Windows (.msi). After download, you can launch them, and they walk you through the installation process.

Prebuilt Linux packages are available from https://github.com/ nxadm/rakudo-pkg/releases/ for Debian, Ubuntu, CentOS, and Fedora.

In both cases, use version 202.01 to get the best compatibility with the examples used in this book.

Note that Rakudo is not relocatable, which means you have to install to a fixed location that was decided by the creator of the installer. Moving the installation to a different directory is not possible.

On Windows, the installer (Figure 2-1) offers to add C:\rakudo\bin and C:\rakudo\share\perl6\site\bin to your PATH environment. You should choose that option, as it allows you to execute Raku (and programs that the module installer installs on your behalf) without specifying full paths.

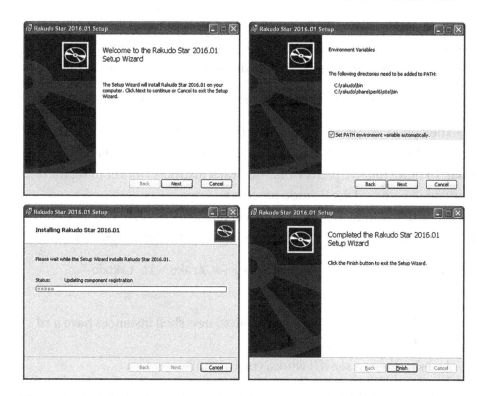

Figure 2-1. *The Rakudo Star installer consists of four easy screens*

2.2 Docker

On platforms that support Docker, you can pull an existing Docker container from the docker hub:

```
$ docker pull rakudo-star:2020.01
```

Then you can get an interactive Rakudo shell with this command:

```
$ docker run -it rakudo-star:2020.01 raku
```

9

But that alone won't work for executing scripts, because the container has its own separate file system. To make scripts available inside the container, you need to tell Docker to make the current directory available to the container:

```
$ docker run -v $PWD:/raku -w /raku -it rakudo-star:2020.01 raku
```

The option -v $PWD:/raku instructs Docker to mount the current working directory ($PWD) into the container, where it'll be available as /raku. To make relative paths work, -w /raku instructs Docker to set the working directory of the Rakudo process to /raku.

Since this command line starts to get unwieldy, I created an alias (this is Bash syntax; other shells might have slightly different alias mechanisms):

```
alias rd='docker run -v $PWD:/raku -w /raku -it rakudo-star:2020.01 raku'
```

I put this line into my ~/.bashrc file so new shell instances have a rd command, short for "Raku docker."

As a short test to see if it works, you can run

```
$ rd -e 'say "hi"'
hi
```

If you go the Docker route, use the rd alias instead of raku to run scripts.

2.3 Building from Source

To build Rakudo Star from source, you need make, the GNU C Compiler[1] (GCC), or clang and Perl 5 installed. This example installs into $HOME/opt/rakudo-star:

```
$ wget https://rakudo.org/dl/star/rakudo-star-2020.01.tar.gz
$ tar xzf rakudo-star-2020.01.tar.gz
```

---

[1]http://gcc.gnu.org/

```
$ cd rakudo-star-2020.01/
$ perl Configure.pl --prefix=$HOME/opt/rakudo-star --gen-moar
$ make install
```

You should have about 2GB of RAM available for the last step; building a compiler is a resource-intensive task.

You need to add paths to two directories to your PATH environment variable, one for Rakudo itself and one for programs installed by the module installer:

```
PATH=$PATH:$HOME/opt/rakudo-star/bin/:$HOME/opt/rakudo-star/
share/perl6/site/bin
```

If you are a Bash user, you can put that line into your ~/.bashrc file to make it available in new Bash processes.

2.4 Testing Your Rakudo Star Installation

You should now be able to run Perl 6 programs from the command line and ask Rakudo for its version:

```
$ raku --version
This is Rakudo version 2020.01 built on MoarVM version
2020.01.1
implementing Perl 6.d.

$ perl6 -e "say <hi>"
hi
```

If, against all odds, all of these approaches have failed to produce a usable Rakudo installation, you should describe your problem to the friendly Raku community, which can usually provide some help. https://raku.org/community/ describes ways to interact with the community.

2.5 Documentation

Rakudo itself has little documentation, since most of the interesting material is about the Raku language. But Rakudo does come with a summary of command-line options that you can access by calling raku `--help`.

The official place for Raku language documentation is at `https://docs.raku.org/`, which aims to provide both reference and tutorial-style material. Other good resources are listed at `https://raku.org/resources/`, many of which are created and maintained by members of the Raku community.

2.6 Summary

On most platforms, you can install Rakudo Star from prebuilt binary installers. Where this doesn't work, Docker images are available. Finally, Rakudo Star can be built from its sources.

CHAPTER 3

Formatting a Sudoku Puzzle

As a gentle introduction to Raku, let's consider a small task that I recently encountered while pursuing one of my hobbies.

Sudoku is a number placement puzzle played on a grid of 9×9 cells, subdivided into blocks of 3×3 (Figure 3-1). Some of the cells are filled out with numbers from 1 to 9; some are empty. The objective of the game is to fill out the empty cells so that in each row, column, and 3×3 block, each digit from 1 to 9 occurs exactly once.

Figure 3-1. *A Sudoku puzzle in its unsolved form*

© Moritz Lenz 2020
M. Lenz, *Raku Fundamentals*, https://doi.org/10.1007/978-1-4842-6109-5_3

An efficient storage format for a Sudoku is simply a string of 81 characters, with 0 for empty cells and the digits 1 to 9 for prefilled cells. The task I want to solve is to bring this into a friendlier format.

The input could be

000000075000080094000500600010002000090005700600304000100002 3080000006063240000

On to our first Raku program:

```
# file sudoku.p6
use v6.d;
my $sudoku = '000000075000080094000500600010002000009000570060
03040001000023080000006063240000';
for 0..8 -> $line-number {
    say substr $sudoku, $line-number * 9, 9;
}
```

You can run it like this:

```
$ perl6 sudoku.p6
000000075
000080094
000500600
010000200
000900057
006003040
001000023
080000006
063240000
```

There's not much magic in there, but let's go through the code one line at a time. The first line, starting with a #, is a comment that extends to the end of the line.

```
use v6.d;
```

This line is not strictly necessary, but good practice anyway. It declares the Raku version you are using, here v6.d.

The 6 in the version is a heritage from the days when Raku was Perl 6, and v6.d is the current version at the time of writing (March of 2020).

The first interesting line is

```
my $sudoku = '00000007500...';
```

my declares a lexical variable. It is visible from the point of the declaration to the end of the current scope, which means either to the end of the current block delimited by curly braces or to the end of the file if it's outside any block, as it is in this example.

Variables start with a *sigil*, here a $. Sigils are what gave Perl the reputation of being line noise, but there is signal in the noise. The $ looks like an S, which stands for *scalar*. If you know some math, you know that a scalar is just a single value, as opposed to a vector or even a matrix.

This variable doesn't start its life empty, because there's an initialization right next to it. The value it starts with is a string literal, as indicated by the quotes.

Note that there is no need to declare the type of the variable beyond the very vague "it's a scalar" implied by the sigil. If we wanted, we could add a type constraint:

```
my Str $sudoku = '00000007500...';
```

But when quickly prototyping, I tend to forego type constraints, because I often don't know yet how exactly the code will work out.

The actual logic happens in the next lines, by iterating over the line numbers 0 to 8:

```
for 0..8 -> $line-number {
    ...
}
```

The `for` loop has the general structure `for ITERABLE BLOCK`. Here the iterable is a range,[1] and the block is a *pointy block, an anonymous piece of code with a signature. Some other languages call this a lambda.* The block starts with `->`, which introduces a *signature*. The signature tells the compiler what arguments the block expects, here a single scalar called `$line-number`. The variable from the signature, $line-number, is visible from the point of the declaration until the closing curly brace of the block. In the signature, you can include optional type constraints, like this: `for 0..8 -> Int $line-number { ... }.`

You might have noticed that the variable name, $line-number, contains a dash. Raku allows the use of dash `-` or a single quote `'` to join multiple simple identifiers into a larger identifier. That means you can use them inside an identifier as long as the following character is a letter or an underscore.

```
say substr $sudoku, $line-number * 9, 9;
```

Both say[2] and substr[3] are functions provided by the Raku standard library. `substr($string, $from, $num-chars)` extracts a substring from `$string`. It starts from a zero-based index `$from` and takes the number of characters specified by `$num-chars`. Oh, and in Raku one character is truly one character, even if it is made up of multiple code points like an accented Roman letter.

say then prints this substring, followed by a line break.

As you can see from the example, function invocations don't need parentheses, though you can add them if you want:

```
say substr($sudoku, $line-number * 9, 9);
```

or even

```
say(substr($sudoku, $line-number * 9, 9));
```

---

[1] https://docs.raku.org/type/Range.html
[2] https://docs.raku.org/routine/say# (IO)_sub_say
[3] https://docs.raku.org/type/Str#routine_substr

3.1 Making the Sudoku Playable

As the output of our script stands now, you can't play the resulting Sudoku even if you printed it on paper. All those pesky zeros get in the way of actually entering your carefully deduced numbers!

So, let's substitute each 0 with a blank so you can solve the puzzle:

```
# file sudoku.p6
use v6;

my $sudoku = '000000075000080094000500600010000200009000570060
030400010000230800000006063240000';
$sudoku = $sudoku.trans('0' => ' ');

for 0..8 -> $line-number {
    say substr $sudoku, $line-number * 9, 9;
}
```

trans[4] is a method of the Str class. Its argument is a Pair.[5] The boring way to create a Pair would be Pair.new('0', ' '), but since it's so commonly used, there is a shortcut in the form of the *fat arrow*, =>. The method trans replaces each occurrence of the pair's key with the pair's value and returns the resulting string.

Speaking of shortcuts, you can also shorten $sudoku = $sudoku.trans(...) to $sudoku.=trans(...). This is a general pattern that turns methods that return a result into mutators.

---

[4]https://docs.raku.org/type/Str.html#method_trans
[5]https://docs.raku.org/type/Pair

With the new string substitution, the result is playable but ugly:

```
$ perl6 sudoku.p6
        75
    8   94
    5 6
1     2
    9   57
    6 3 4
    1   23
8       6
6324
```

A bit of ASCII art makes it bearable:

```
+---+---+---+
|   | 1 |   |
|   |   |79 |
| 9 |   | 4 |
+---+---+---+
|   | 4|  5|
|   |   | 2 |
|3  | 29|18 |
+---+---+---+
|  4| 87|2  |
|  7|  2|95 |
| 5 |  3|  8|
+---+---+---+
```

To get the vertical dividing lines, we need to subdivide the lines into smaller chunks. And since we already have one occurrence of dividing a string into smaller strings of a fixed size, it's time to encapsulate it into a function:

```
sub chunks(Str $s, Int $chars) {
    gather loop (my $idx = 0; $idx < $s.chars; $idx += $chars)
{
        take substr($s, $idx, $chars);
    }
}

for chunks($sudoku, 9) -> $line {
    say chunks($line, 3).join('|');
}
```

The output is

```
$ perl6 sudoku.p6
  |   | 75
  | 8 | 94
  |5  |6
 1 |   |2
  |9 | 57
  6|  3| 4
  1|   | 23
 8 |   |  6
 63|24 |
```

But how did it work? Well, sub (SIGNATURE) BLOCK declares a
subroutine, short *sub*. Here I declare it to take two arguments, and since I
tend to confuse the order of arguments to functions I call, I've added type
constraints to make it very likely that Raku catches the error for me.

gather and take work together to create a list. gather is the entry
point, and each execution of take adds one element to the list. So

```
gather {
    take 1;
    take 2;
}
```

would return the list 1, 2. Here gather acts as a statement prefix, which means it collects all takes from within the loop.

The loop statement takes the form loop (INITIAL, CONDITION, POST) BLOCK and works like a for loop in C and related languages. It first executes INITIAL, and then while CONDITION is true, first executes the BLOCK and then executesPOST.

A subroutine returns the value from the last expression,[6] which here is the gather loop ... construct discussed above.

Coming back to the program, the for loop now looks like this:

```
for chunks($sudoku, 9) -> $line {
    say chunks($line, 3).join('|');
}
```

First the program chops up the full Sudoku string into lines of nine characters and then for each line chops it up again into a list of three strings each with a length of three characters. The join method[7] turns it back into a string but with pipe symbols inserted between the chunks.

There are still vertical bars missing at the start and end of the line, which can easily be hard-coded by changing the last line:

```
say '|', chunks($line, 3).join('|'), '|';
```

Now the output is

```
|   |   | 75|
|   | 8 | 94|
|   |5  |6  |
| 1 |   |2  |
|   |9  | 57|
```

---

[6]You can also use return EXPRESSION to return a value and exit the subroutine immediately.

[7]https://docs.raku.org/type/List#routine_join

```
|  6|  3| 4 |
|  1|   | 23|
| 8 |   | 6|
| 63|24 |   |
```

Only the horizontal lines are missing, which aren't too hard to add:

```
my $separator = '+---+---+---+';
my $index = 0;
for chunks($sudoku, 9) -> $line {
    if $index++ %% 3 {
        say $separator;
    }
    say '|', chunks($line, 3).join('|'), '|';
}
say $separator;
```

Et voilà:

```
+---+---+---+
|   |   | 75|
|   | 8 | 94|
|   |5  |6  |
+---+---+---+
| 1 |   |2  |
|   |9  | 57|
|  6|  3| 4 |
+---+---+---+
|  1|   | 23|
| 8 |   | 6|
| 63|24 |   |
+---+---+---+
```

There are some new aspects here: the if conditional, which structurally very much resembles the for loop, and the divisibility operator, %%. From other programming languages you probably know % for modulo, but since $number % $divisor == 0 is such a common pattern, $number %% $divisor is Raku's shortcut for it.

Finally, you might know the ++ postfix operator from programming languages such as C or Perl 5. It increments the variable by one but returns the old value, so

```
my $x = 0;
say $x++;
say $x;
```

first prints 0 and then 1. Just like in many other programming languages, you can apply the ++ as prefix operator, in which case it increments and returns the incremented value.

3.2 Shortcuts, Constants, and More Shortcuts

Raku is modeled after human languages, which have some kind of compression scheme built in, where commonly used words tend to be short and common constructs have shortcuts.

As such, there are lots of ways to write the code more succinctly. The first is basically cheating, because the sub-chunks can be replaced by a built-in method in the Str class, comb[8]:

---

[8]https://docs.raku.org/type/Str#routine_comb

```
# file sudoku.p6
use v6;
my $sudoku = '0000000750000800940005006000100002000009000570060
0304000100002308000000606324000';
$sudoku = $sudoku.trans('0' => ' ');

my $separator = '+---+---+---+';
my $index = 0;
for $sudoku.comb(9) -> $line {
    if $index++ %% 3 {
        say $separator;
    }
    say '|', $line.comb(3).join('|'), '|';
}
say $separator;
```

The if conditional can be applied as a statement postfix:

```
say $separator if $index++ %% 3;
```

Except for the initialization, the variable $index is used only once, so there's no need to give it a name. Yes, Raku has anonymous variables:

```
my $separator = '+---+---+---+';
for $sudoku.comb(9) -> $line {
    say $separator if $++ %% 3;
    say '|', $line.comb(3).join('|'), '|';
}
say $separator;
```

Since $separator is a constant, we can declare it as one:

```
constant $separator = '+---+---+---+';
```

If you want to reduce the line noise factor, you can also forego the sigil, so constant separator = '...'.

Finally, there is another syntax for method calls with arguments: instead of $obj.method(args) you can say $obj.method: args, which brings us to the idiomatic form of the small Sudoku formatter:

```
# file sudoku.p6
use v6.d;
my $sudoku = '000000075000080094000500600010002000009000570060
0304000100002308000006063240000';
$sudoku = $sudoku.trans: '0' => ' ';

constant separator = '+---+---+---+';
for $sudoku.comb(9) -> $line {
    say separator if $++ %% 3;
    say '|', $line.comb(3).join('|'), '|';
}
say separator;
```

The output remains unchanged by these changes to the Raku code.

3.3 I/O and Other Tragedies

A practical script doesn't contain its input as a hard-coded string literal but reads it from the command line, standard input, or a file.

If you want to read the Sudoku from the command line, you can declare a subroutine called MAIN, which gets all command-line arguments passed in:

```
# file sudoku.p6
use v6.d;
constant separator = '+---+---+---+';

sub MAIN($sudoku) {
    my $substituted = $sudoku.trans: '0' => ' ';
```

```
for $substituted.comb(9) -> $line {
    say separator if $++ %% 3;
    say '|', $line.comb(3).join('|'), '|';
}
say separator;
}
```

This is how it's called:

```
$ perl6 sudoku.p6 000000075000080094000500600010000200000900057
006003040001000023080000006063240000
+---+---+---+
|   |   | 75|
|   | 8 | 94|
|   |5  |6  |
+---+---+---+
| 1 |   |2  |
|   |9  | 57|
|  6|  3| 4 |
+---+---+---+
|  1|   | 23|
| 8 |   |  6|
| 63|24 |   |
+---+---+---+
```

And you even get a usage message for free if you use it incorrectly, for example, by omitting the argument:

```
$ perl6 sudoku.p6
Usage:
  sudoku.p6 <sudoku>
```

You might have noticed that the last example uses a separate variable for the substituted Sudoku string. This is because function parameters (aka variables declared in a signature) are read-only by default. Instead of creating a new variable, I could have also written sub MAIN($sudoku is copy) { ... }.

Classic UNIX programs, such as cat and wc, follow the convention of reading their input from file names given on the command line, or from standard input if no file names are given on the command line.

If you want your program to follow this convention, lines() provides a stream of lines from either of these sources:

```
# file sudoku.p6
use v6.d;

constant separator = '+---+---+---+';

for lines() -> $sudoku {
    my $substituted = $sudoku.trans: '0' => ' ';

    for $substituted.comb(9) -> $line {
        say separator if $++ %% 3;
        say '|', $line.comb(3).join('|'), '|';
    }
    say separator;

}
```

3.4 Get Creative!

You won't learn a programming language from reading a book; you have to actually use it—tinker with it. If you want to expand on the examples discussed earlier, I'd encourage you to try to produce Sudokus in different output formats.

SVG[9] is a text-based vector graphics format that offers all the primitives necessary for rendering a Sudoku: rectangles, lines, text, and much more. You can use it if you want to achieve relatively good output with little effort.

This is the rough skeleton of an SVG file for a Sudoku:

```
<?xml version="1.0" standalone="no"?>
<!DOCTYPE svg PUBLIC "-//W3C//DTD SVG 1.1//EN"
"http://www.w3.org/Graphics/SVG/1.1/DTD/svg11.dtd">
<svg width="304" height="304" version="1.1"
xmlns="http://www.w3.org/2000/svg">
    <line x1="0" x2="300" y1="33.3333" y2="33.3333"
    style="stroke:grey" />
    <line x1="0" x2="300" y1="66.6667" y2="66.6667"
    style="stroke:grey" />
    <line x1="0" x2="303" y1="100" y2="100"
    style="stroke:black;stroke-width:2" />
    <line x1="0" x2="300" y1="133.333" y2="133.333"
    style="stroke:grey" />
    <!-- more horizontal lines here -->
    <line y1="0" y2="300" x1="33.3333" x2="33.3333"
    style="stroke:grey" />
    <!-- more vertical lines here -->

    <text x="43.7333" y="124.5"> 1 </text>
    <text x="43.7333" y="257.833"> 8 </text>
    <!-- more cells go here -->
    <rect width="304" height="304" style="fill:none;stroke-
    width:1;stroke:black;stroke-width:6"/>
</svg>
```

9https://en.wikipedia.org/wiki/Scalable_Vector_Graphics

If you have a Firefox or Chrome browser or a dedicated vector graphics program such as Inkscape,[10] you can use it to open the SVG file (Figure 3-2).

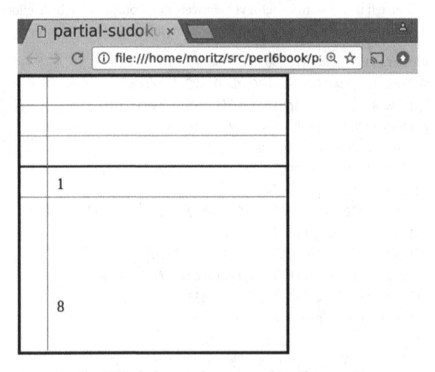

Figure 3-2. *The SVG skeleton when viewed in Chrome. You can see the placement of both of the grid lines and of some initial letters*

3.5 Summary

The first Raku example introduced literals, variables, and control flow. We have seen that Raku borrows many concepts from other languages such as lambdas, the ++ postfix operator, and common control flow like if and for. Some of the features are more unusual, like the MAIN subroutine whose signature is automatically translated to a command-line argument parser.

---

[10]https://inkscape.org/

We have also seen that Raku often offers multiple ways to the same thing, leaving you room to express both the focus of your program and yourself. The Perl and Raku communities often call this *There is more than one way to do it*, abbreviated Timtowtdi.

CHAPTER 4

Datetime Conversion for the Command Line

Occasionally I work with a database that stores dates and datetimes as UNIX timestamps, a.k.a. the number of seconds since midnight 1970-01-01. Unlike the original author of the database and surrounding code, I cannot convert between UNIX timestamps and human-readable date formats in my head, so I write tools for that.

Our goal here is to write a small tool that converts back and forth between UNIX timestamps and dates/times:

```
$ autotime 2015-12-24
1450915200
$ autotime 2015-12-24 11:23:00
1450956180
$ autotime 1450915200
2015-12-24
$ autotime 1450956180
2015-12-24 11:23:00
```

© Moritz Lenz 2020
M. Lenz, *Raku Fundamentals*, https://doi.org/10.1007/978-1-4842-6109-5_4

4.1 Libraries to the Rescue

Date and time arithmetic is surprisingly hard to get right, and at the same time rather boring; hence, I'm happy to delegate that part to libraries.

Raku ships with DateTime[1] (somewhat inspired by the Perl 5 module of the same name) and Date[2] (mostly blatantly stolen from Perl 5's Date::Simple module) in the core library. These two will handle the actual conversions. Our focus will be on creating a friendly user experience for the input and output of the conversions.

For the conversion from a UNIX timestamp to a date or datetime, the DateTime.new constructor comes in handy. It has a variant that accepts a single integer as a UNIX timestamp:

```
$ perl6 -e "say DateTime.new(1450915200)"
2015-12-24T00:00:00Z
```

Looks like we're almost done with one direction, right?

```
#!/usr/bin/env raku
use v6.d;
sub MAIN(Int $timestamp) {
    say DateTime.new($timestamp)
}
```

Let's run it:

```
$ autotime 1450915200
Invalid DateTime string '1450915200'; use an ISO 8601 timestamp
(yyyy-mm-ddThh:mm:ssZ or yyyy-mm-ddThh:mm:ss+01:00) instead
  in sub MAIN at autotime line 2
  in block <unit> at autotime line 2
```

---

[1]https://docs.raku.org/type/DateTime
[2]https://docs.raku.org/type/Date

Oh no, what happened? It seems that the DateTime constructor views the argument as a string, even though the parameter to sub MAIN is declared as an Int. How can that be? Let's add some debugging output:

```
#!/usr/bin/env raku
use v6.d;
sub MAIN(Int $timestamp) {
    say $timestamp.^name;
    say DateTime.new($timestamp)
}
```

Running it now with the same invocation as before, there's an extra line of output before the error:

```
IntStr
```

$thing.^name is a call to a method of the meta class of $thing, and name asks it for its name (in other words, the name of the class). IntStr[3] is a subclass of both Int and Str, which is why the DateTime constructor legitimately considers it a Str. The mechanism that parses command-line arguments before they are passed on to MAIN converts the string from the command line to IntStr instead of Str, in order to not lose information in case we do want to treat it as a string.

Cutting a long story short, we can force the argument into a "real" integer by adding a + prefix, which is the general mechanism for conversion to a numeric value:

```
#!/usr/bin/env perl6
sub MAIN(Int $timestamp) {
    say DateTime.new(+$timestamp)
}
```

---

[3]https://docs.raku.org/type/IntStr

A quick test shows that it now works:

```
$ ./autotime-01.p6 1450915200
2015-12-24T00:00:00Z
```

The output is in the ISO 8601 timestamp format,[4] which might not be the easiest on the eye. For a date (when hour, minute, and second are zero), we really want just the date:

```
#!/usr/bin/env perl6
sub MAIN(Int $timestamp) {
    my $dt = DateTime.new(+$timestamp);
    if $dt.hour == 0 && $dt.minute == 0 && $dt.second == 0 {
        say $dt.Date;
    }
    else {
        say $dt;
    }
}
```

Better:

```
$ ./autotime 1450915200
2015-12-24
```

But the conditional is a bit clunky. Really, three comparisons to 0? Raku has a neat little feature that lets you write this more compactly:

```
if all($dt.hour, $dt.minute, $dt.second) == 0 {
    say $dt.Date;
}
```

---

[4]www.iso.org/iso-8601-date-and-time-format.html

all(...) creates a *Junction*,[5] a composite value of several other values, that also stores a logical mode. When you compare a junction to another value, that comparison automatically applies to all the values in the junction. The if statement evaluates the junction in a boolean context, and in this case only returns True if all comparisons returned True as well.

Other types of junctions exist: any, all, none, and one. Considering that 0 is the only integer that is false in a boolean context, we could even write the preceding statement as

```
if none($dt.hour, $dt.minute, $dt.second) {
    say $dt.Date;
}
```

Neat, right?

But you don't always need fancy language constructs to write concise programs. In this case, approaching the problem from a slightly different angle yields even shorter and clearer code. If the DateTime object round-trips a conversion to Date and back to DateTime without loss of information, it's clearly a Date:

```
if $dt.Date.DateTime == $dt {
    say $dt.Date;
}
else {
    say $dt;
}
```

Another way we could truncate the DateTime object is using the truncated-to method:

```
if $dt.truncated-to('day') == $dt {
    say $dt.Date;
}
```

---

[5]https://docs.raku.org/type/Junction

```
else {
    say $dt;
}
```

4.2 DateTime Formatting

For a timestamp that doesn't resolve to a full day, the output from our script currently looks like this:

```
2015-12-24T00:00:01Z
```

where "Z" indicates the UTC or "Zulu" timezone.

Instead I'd like it to be

```
2015-12-24 00:00:01
```

The `DateTime` class supports custom formatters, so let's write one:

```
sub MAIN(Int $timestamp) {
    my $dt = DateTime.new(+$timestamp, formatter => sub ($o) {
            sprintf '%04d-%02d-%02d %02d:%02d:%02d',
                    $o.year, $o.month, $o.day,
                    $o.hour, $o.minute, $o.second,
    });
    if $dt.Date.DateTime == $dt {
        say $dt.Date;
    }
    else {
        say $dt.Str;
    }
}
```

Now the output looks better:

```
./autotime 1450915201
2015-12-24 00:00:01
```

You can replace the format string with your own if you want to produce output in a different format, like DD.MM.YYYY.

The syntax formatter => ... in the context of an argument denotes a named argument, which means the name and not the position in the argument list decides which parameter to bind to. This is very handy if there are a bunch of parameters.

Let's consider the function

```
sub cuboid(:$width, :$height, :$depth) {
    say "Width: $width, Height: $height, Depth: $depth";
}
```

you could call that as

```
cuboid( width  => 5, height => 8, depth => 2 )
```

or

```
cuboid( depth => 2, width  => 5, height => 8 )
```

or any other permutation of arguments, all producing the same output.

Another syntax for passing named arguments is the colonpair notation:

```
cuboid( :depth(2), :width(5), :height(8) )
```

Returning to the DateTime formatting, I don't like the code anymore, because the formatter is inline in the DateTime.new(...) call, which I find unclear.

Let's make this a separate routine:

```
#!/usr/bin/env perl6
sub MAIN(Int $timestamp) {
    sub formatter($o) {
        sprintf '%04d-%02d-%02d %02d:%02d:%02d',
                $o.year, $o.month, $o.day,
                $o.hour, $o.minute, $o.second,
    }
```

```
my $dt = DateTime.new(+$timestamp, formatter =>
&formatter);
if $dt.Date.DateTime == $dt {
    say $dt.Date;
}
else {
    say $dt.Str;
}
}
```

Yes, you can put a subroutine declaration inside the body of another subroutine declaration; a subroutine is just an ordinary lexical symbol, like a variable declared with my.

In the line my $dt = DateTime.new(+$timestamp, formatter => &formatter);, the syntax &formatter refers to the subroutine as an object, without calling it.

This being Raku, formatter => &formatter has a shortcut: :&formatter. As a general rule, if you want to fill a named parameter whose name is the name of a variable, and whose value is the value of the variable, you can create it by writing :$variable. And by extension, :thing is short for thing => True.

4.3 Looking the Other Way

Now that the conversion from timestamps to dates and times works fine, let's look in the other direction. Our small tool needs to parse the input and decide whether the input is a timestamp or a date and optionally a time.

The boring way would be to use a conditional:

```
sub MAIN($input) {
    if $input ~~ / ^ \d+ $ / {
        # convert from timestamp to date/datetime
    }
```

```
else {
    # convert from date to timestamp

}
}
```

But I hate boring, so I want to look at a more exciting (and extensible) approach.

Raku supports multiple dispatch. That means you can have multiple subroutines with the same name but different signatures. And Raku automatically decides which one to call. You have to explicitly enable this feature by writing multi sub instead of sub, so that Raku can catch accidental redeclaration for you.

```
#!/usr/bin/env perl6

multi sub MAIN(Int $timestamp) {
    sub formatter($o) {
        sprintf '%04d-%02d-%02d %02d:%02d:%02d',
                $o.year, $o.month, $o.day,
                $o.hour, $o.minute, $o.second,
    }
    my $dt = DateTime.new(+$timestamp, :&formatter);
    if $dt.Date.DateTime == $dt {
        say $dt.Date;
    }
    else {
        say $dt.Str;
    }
}

multi sub MAIN(Str $date) {
    say Date.new($date).DateTime.posix
}
```

Let's see it in action:

```
$ ./autotime 2015-12-24
1450915200
$ ./autotime 1450915200
Ambiguous call to 'MAIN'; these signatures all match:
:(Int $timestamp)
:(Str $date)
  in block <unit> at ./autotime line 17
```

Not quite what I had envisioned. The problem is again that the integer argument is converted automatically to IntStr and both the Int and the Str multi (or *candidate*) accept that as an argument.

The easiest approach to avoiding this error is narrowing down the kinds of strings that the Str candidate accepts. The classical approach would be to have a regex that roughly validates the incoming argument:

```
multi sub MAIN(Str $date where /^ \d+ \- \d+ \- \d+ $ /) {
    say Date.new($date).DateTime.posix
}
```

And indeed it works, but why duplicate the logic that Date.new already has for validating date strings? If you pass a string argument that doesn't look like a date, you get an error like this:

```
Invalid Date string 'foobar'; use yyyy-mm-dd instead
```

We can use this behavior to constrain the string parameter of the MAIN multi candidate:

```
multi sub MAIN(Str $date where { try Date.new($_) }) {
    say Date.new($date).DateTime.posix
}
```

The additional try in here is because subtype constraints behind a where are not supposed to throw an exception, just return a false value.

And now it works as intended:

```
$ ./autotime 2015-12-24;
1450915200
$ ./autotime 1450915200
2015-12-24
```

4.4 Dealing with Time

The only feature left to implement is conversion of date and time to a timestamp. In other words, we want to handle calls like autotime 2015-12-24 11:23:00:

```
multi sub MAIN(Str $date where { try Date.new($_) }, Str
$time?) {
    my $d = Date.new($date);
    if $time {
        my ( $hour, $minute, $second ) = $time.split(':');
        say DateTime.new(date => $d, :$hour, :$minute,
        :$second).posix;
    }
    else {
        say $d.DateTime.posix;
    }
}
```

The new second argument is optional by virtue of the trailing ?. If it is present, we split the time string on the colon to get hour, minute, and second. My first instinct while writing this code was to use shorter variable names, my ($h, $m, $s) = $time.split(':'), but then the call to the DateTime constructor would have looked like this:

```
DateTime.new(date => $d, hour => $h, minute => $m, second => $s);
```

41

So the named arguments to the constructor made me choose more self-explanatory variable names.

So, this works:

```
./autotime 2015-12-24 11:23:00
1450956180
```

And we can check that it round-trips:

```
$ ./autotime 1450956180
2015-12-24 11:23:00
```

4.5 Tighten Your Seat Belt

Now that the program is feature complete, we should strive to remove some clutter, and explore a few more awesome Raku features.

The first feature that I want to exploit is that of an *implicit variable* or *topic*. A quick demonstration:

```
for 1..3 {
    .say
}
```

produces the output

```
1
2
3
```

There is no explicit iteration variable, so Raku implicitly binds the current value of the loop to a variable called $_. The method call .say is a shortcut for $_.say. And since there is a subroutine that calls six methods on the same variable, using $_ here is a nice visual optimization:

```
sub formatter($_) {
    sprintf '%04d-%02d-%02d %02d:%02d:%02d',
            .year, .month, .day,
            .hour, .minute, .second,
}
```

If you want to set $_ in a lexical scope without resorting to a function definition, you can use the given VALUE BLOCK construct:

```
given DateTime.new(+$timestamp, :&formatter) {
    if .Date.DateTime == $_ {
        say .Date;
    }
    else {
        .say;
    }
}
```

And Raku also offers a shortcut for conditionals on the $_ variable, which can be used as a generalized switch statement:

```
given DateTime.new(+$timestamp, :&formatter) {
    when .Date.DateTime == $_ { say .Date }
    default { .say }
}
```

If you have a read-only variable or parameter, you can do without the $ sigil, though you have to use a backslash at declaration time:

```
multi sub MAIN(Int \timestamp) {
    ...
    given DateTime.new(+timestamp, :&formatter) {
    ...
    }
}
```

So now the full code looks like this:

```perl6
#!/usr/bin/env perl6

multi sub MAIN(Int \timestamp) {
    sub formatter($_) {
        sprintf '%04d-%02d-%02d %02d:%02d:%02d',
                .year, .month, .day,
                .hour, .minute, .second,
    }
    given DateTime.new(+timestamp, :&formatter) {
        when .Date.DateTime == $_ { say .Date }
        default { .say }
    }
}

multi sub MAIN(Str $date where { try Date.new($_) }, Str
$time?) {
    my $d = Date.new($date);
    if $time {
        my ( $hour, $minute, $second ) = $time.split(':');
        say DateTime.new(date => $d, :$hour, :$minute,
        :$second).posix;
    }
    else {
        say $d.DateTime.posix;
    }
}
```

4.6 MAIN Magic

The magic that calls sub MAIN for us also provides us with an automagic usage message if we call it with arguments that don't fit any multi; for instance with no arguments at all:

```
$ ./autotime
Usage:
  ./autotime <timestamp>
  ./autotime <date> [<time>]
```

We can add a short description to these usage lines by adding semantic comments before the MAIN subs:

```
#!/usr/bin/env perl6

#| Convert timestamp to ISO date
multi sub MAIN(Int \timestamp) {
    ...
}

#| Convert ISO date to timestamp
multi sub MAIN(Str $date where { try Date.new($_) }, Str
$time?) {
    ...
}
```

Now the usage message becomes

```
$ ./autotime
Usage:
  ./autotime <timestamp> -- Convert timestamp to ISO date
  ./autotime <date> [<time>] -- Convert ISO date to timestamp
```

4.7 Automated Tests

We've seen some code go through several iterations of refactoring.
Refactoring without automated tests tends to make me uneasy, so I
actually had a small shell script that called the script under development
with several different argument combinations and compared it to an
expected result.

Let's now look at a way to write test code in Raku itself.

In the Raku community, it's common to move logic into modules to
make it easier to test with external test scripts, but for small tools such as
this, I prefer to stick with a single file containing code and tests and to run
the tests via a separate test command.

To make testing easier, let's first separate I/O from the application
logic:

```
#!/usr/bin/env Raku6

sub from-timestamp(Int \timestamp) {
    sub formatter($_) {
        sprintf '%04d-%02d-%02d %02d:%02d:%02d',
                .year, .month, .day,
                .hour, .minute, .second,
    }
    given DateTime.new(+timestamp, :&formatter) {
        when .Date.DateTime == $_ { return .Date }
        default { return $_ }
    }
}

sub from-date-string(Str $date, Str $time?) {
    my $d = Date.new($date);
    if $time {
```

```
        my ( $hour, $minute, $second ) = $time.split(':');
        return DateTime.new(date => $d, :$hour, :$minute,
        :$second);
    }
    else {
        return $d.DateTime;
    }
}

#| Convert timestamp to ISO date
multi sub MAIN(Int \timestamp) {
    say from-timestamp(+timestamp);
}
#| Convert ISO date to timestamp
multi sub MAIN(Str $date where { try Date.new($_) }, Str
$time?) {
    say from-date-string($date, $time).posix;
}
```

With this small refactoring out of the way, let's add some tests:

```
#| Run internal tests
multi sub MAIN('test') {
    use Test;
    plan 4;
    is-deeply from-timestamp(1450915200), Date.new('2015-
    12-24'),
        'Timestamp to Date';;
    my $dt = from-timestamp(1450915201);
    is $dt, "2015-12-24 00:00:01",
        'Timestamp to DateTime with string formatting';

    is from-date-string('2015-12-24').posix, 1450915200,
        'from-date-string, one argument';
```

```
  is from-date-string('2015-12-24', '00:00:01').posix,
  1450915201,
      'from-date-string, two arguments';
}
```

And you can run it:

```
./autotime test
1..4
ok 1 - Timestamp to Date
ok 2 - Timestamp to DateTime with string formatting
ok 3 - from-date-string, one argument
ok 4 - from-date-string, two arguments
```

The output format is that of the Test Anything Protocol (TAP),[6] which is the de facto standard in the Raku community[7] but is now also used in other communities. For larger output strings, it is a good idea to run the tests through a test harness. For our four lines of test output, this isn't yet necessary, but if you want to do that anyway, you can use the prove program that's shipped with Perl 5:

```
$ prove -e "" "./autotime test"
./autotime-tested.p6 test .. ok
All tests successful.
Files=1, Tests=4, 0 wallclock secs ( 0.02 usr 0.01 sys + 0.23
cusr 0.02 csys = 0.28 CPU)
Result: PASS
```

In a terminal, this even colors the "All tests successful" output in green, to make it easier to spot. Test failures are marked up in red.

---

[6]https://testanything.org/

[7]http://testanything.org/testing-with-tap/Raku.html

How does the testing work? The first line of code uses a new feature we haven't seen yet:

```
multi sub MAIN('test') {
```

What's that, a literal instead of a parameter in the subroutine signature? That's right. And it's a shortcut for

```
multi sub MAIN(Str $anon where {$anon eq 'test'}) {
```

except that it does not declare the variable $anon. So it's a multi candidate that you can only call by supplying the string 'test' as the sole argument.

The next line, use Test;, loads the test module[8] that's shipped with Rakudo. It also imports into the current lexical scope all the symbols that Test exports by default. This includes the functions plan, is, and is-deeply that are used later on.

plan 4; declares that we want to run four tests. This is useful for detecting unplanned, early exits from the test code or errors in looping logic in the test code that leads to running fewer tests than planned. If you can't be bothered to count your tests in advance, you can leave out the plan call, and instead call done-testing after your tests are done.

Both is-deeply and is expect the value to be tested as the first argument, the expected value as the second argument, and an optional test label string as the third argument. The difference is that is() compares the first two arguments as strings, whereas is-deeply uses a deep equality comparison logic using the eqv operator.[9] Such tests only pass if the two arguments are of the same type and recursively are (or contain) the same values.

---

[8]https://docs.raku.org/language/testing
[9]https://docs.raku.org/routine/eqv

More testing functions are available, like ok(), which succeeds for a true argument, and nok(), which expects a false argument. You can also nest tests with subtest:

```
#| Run internal tests
multi sub MAIN('test') {
    use Test;
    plan 2;
    subtest 'timestamp', {
        plan 2;
        is-deeply from-timestamp(1450915200), Date.
        new('2015-12-24'),
            'Date';;

        my $dt = from-timestamp(1450915201);
        is $dt, "2015-12-24 00:00:01",
            'DateTime with string formatting';
    };

    subtest 'from-date-string', {
        plan 2;
        is from-date-string('2015-12-24').posix, 1450915200,
            'one argument';
        is from-date-string('2015-12-24', '00:00:01').posix,
        1450915201,
            'two arguments';
    };
}
```

Each call to subtest counts as a single test to the outer test run, so plan 4; has become plan 2;. The subtest call has a test label itself, and then inside a subtest, you have a plan again and calls to test functions as in the following. This is very useful when writing custom test functions that execute a variable number of individual tests.

The output from the nested tests looks like this:

```
1..2
    1..2
    ok 1 - Date
    ok 2 - DateTime with string formatting
ok 1 - timestamp
    1..2
    ok 1 - one argument
    ok 2 - two arguments
ok 2 - from-date-string
```

The test harness now reports just the two top-level tests as the number of run (and passed) tests. And yes, you can nest subtests within subtests, should you really feel the urge to do so.

4.8 Summary

We've seen a bit of Date and DateTime arithmetic, but the exciting part is multiple dispatch; named arguments; subtype constraints with where clauses, given/when, and the implicit $_- variable; and some serious magic when it comes to MAIN subs.

Finally, we learned about automated tests using the Test module that's shipped with Rakudo.

Take some time to read the documentation on what you've worked with so far. See if you can find a place in your code to swap an if for a where[10] statement. Be sure to take advantage of the lexical scope that where introduces.

---

[10]https://docs.raku.org/language/control#with,_orwith,_without

CHAPTER 5

Testing say( )

In the previous chapter, I changed some code so that it wouldn't produce output and instead did the output in the MAIN sub, which conveniently went untested.

Changing code to make it easier to test is a legitimate practice. But if you do have to test code that produces output by calling say, there's a small trick you can use: say works on a file handle, and you can swap out the default file handle, which is connected to standard output. Instead of the default, you can put a dummy file handle in its place that captures the lower-level commands issued to it and record this for testing.

There's a ready-made module for that, IO::String,[1] but for the sake of learning, we'll look at how it works:

```
use v6.d;

# function to be tested
sub doublespeak($x) {
    say $x ~ $x;
}

use Test;
plan 1;
```

---

[1]http://modules.raku.org/dist/IO::String

© Moritz Lenz 2020
M. Lenz, *Raku Fundamentals*, https://doi.org/10.1007/978-1-4842-6109-5_5

```
my class OutputCapture {
    has @!lines;
    method print(\s) {
        @!lines.push(s);
    }
    method captured() {
        @!lines.join;
    }
}

my $output = do {
    my $*OUT = OutputCapture.new;
    doublespeak(42);
    $*OUT.captured;
};

is $output, "4242\n", 'doublespeak works';
```

The first part of the code is the function we want to test, sub doublespeak. It concatenates its argument with itself using the ~ string concatenation operator. The result is passed to say.

Under the hood, say does a bit of formatting and then looks up the variable $*OUT. The * after the sigil marks it as a dynamic variable. The lookup for the dynamic variable goes through the call stack and in each stack frame looks for a declaration of the variable, taking the first it finds. say then calls the method print on that object.

Normally, $*OUT contains an object of type IO::Handle,[2] but the say function doesn't really care about that, as long as it can call a print method on that object. That's called duck typing: we don't really care about the type of the object, as long as it can quack like a duck; or, in this case, print like a duck.

---

[2]https://docs.raku.org/type/IO::Handle

Then comes the loading of the test module,[3] followed by the declaration of how many tests to run:

```
use Test;
plan 1;
```

You can leave out the second line and instead call done-testing after your tests. But if there's a chance that the test code itself might be buggy, and not run tests it's supposed to, it's good to have an upfront declaration of the number of expected tests so that the Test module or the test harness can catch such errors.

The next part of the example is the declaration of a type which we can use to emulate the IO::Handle:

```
my class OutputCapture {
    has @!lines;
    method print(\s) {
        @!lines.push(s);
    }
    method captured() {
        @!lines.join;
    }
}
```

class introduces a class, and the my prefix makes the name lexically scoped, just like in a my $var declaration.

has @!lines declares an attribute, that is, a variable that exists separately for each instance of class OutputCapture. The ! marks it as an attribute. We could leave it out, but having it right there means you always know where the name comes from when reading a larger class.

---

[3]https://docs.raku.org/language/testing.html

The attribute @!lines starts with an @, not a $ as other variables we have seen so far. The @ is the sigil for an array variable.

Sigil	Type Constraint	Default Type	Explanation
$	Mu	Any	Single values and objects
@	Positional	Array	Integer-Indexed compounds
%	Associative	Hash	String- or Object-Indexed compounds
&	Callable		Code objects you can call

You might be seeing a trend now: the first character of a variable or attribute name denotes its rough type (scalar, array, and for routines, and later we'll learn about % for hashes), and if the second character is not a letter, it specifies its scope. We call this second character a *twigil*. So far, we've seen * for dynamic variables and ! for attributes. There are more:

Twigil	Description
*	Dynamically scoped variables
!	Attributes in OO land
^	Implicit positional parameters
:	Implicit named parameters
?	Compiler-provided constants
=	Pod (documentation) variables

The penultimate block of our example is this:

```
my $output = do {
    my $*OUT = OutputCapture.new;
    doublespeak(42);
    $*OUT.captured;
};
```

do { ... } just executes the code inside the curly braces and returns the value of the last statement. Like all code blocks in Raku, it also introduces a new lexical scope.

The new scope comes in handy in the next line, where my $*OUT declares a new dynamic variable $*OUT, which is, however, only valid in the scope of the block. It is initialized with OutputCapture.new, a new instance of the class declared earlier. new isn't magic; it's simply inherited from OutputCapture's superclass. We didn't declare one, but by default, classes get type Any[4] as a superclass, which provides (among other things) the method new as a constructor.

The call to doublespeak calls say, which in turn calls $*OUT.print. And since $*OUT is an instance of OutputCapture in this dynamic scope, the string passed to say lands in OutputCapture's attribute @!lines, where $*OUT.captured can access it again.

The final line

```
is $output, "4242\n", 'doublespeak works';
```

calls the is function from the Test module.

In good old testing tradition, this produces output in the TAP format:

```
1..1
ok 1 - doublespeak works
```

5.1 Summary

We've seen that say( ) uses a dynamically scoped variable, $*OUT, as its output file handle. For testing purposes, we can substitute that with an object of our making, which made us stumble upon the first glimpses of how classes are written in Raku.

---

[4]https://docs.raku.org/type/Any

CHAPTER 6

Silent-Cron: A Cron Wrapper

On Linux and UNIX-like systems, a program called cron[1] periodically executes user-defined commands in the background, according to schedules defined by the user. It is used for system maintenance tasks such as refreshing or removing caches, rotating and deleting old log files, and so on.

If such a command produces any output, cron typically sends an email containing the output so that an admin can look at it and judge if some action is required.

But not all command-line programs are written for usage with cron. For instance, they might produce output even on successful execution and indicate failure through a nonzero exit code. Or they might hang or otherwise misbehave.

To deal with such commands, we'll develop a small program called silent-cron, which wraps such commands and suppresses output when the exit code is zero. It also allows you to specify a timeout that kills the wrapped program if it takes too long:

```
$ silent-cron -- command-that-might-fail args
$ silent-cron --timeout=5 -- command-that-might-hang
```

---

[1]https://en.wikipedia.org/wiki/Cron

© Moritz Lenz 2020

M. Lenz, *Raku Fundamentals*, https://doi.org/10.1007/978-1-4842-6109-5_6

6.1 Running Commands Asynchronously

When you want to run external commands, Raku gives you basically two choices: run,[2] a simple, synchronous interface; and Proc::Async,[3] an asynchronous and slightly more complex option. Even though we will omit the timeout in the first iteration, we need to be aware that implementing the timeout is easier in the asynchronous interface, so that's what we'll use:

```
#!/usr/bin/env perl6

sub MAIN(*@cmd) {
    my $proc = Proc::Async.new(|@cmd);
    my $collector = Channel.new;
    for $proc.stdout, $proc.stderr -> $supply {
        $supply.tap: { $collector.send($_) }
    }
    my $result = $proc.start.result;
    $collector.close;
    my $output = $collector.list.join;
    my $exitcode = $result.exitcode;
    if $exitcode != 0 {
        say "Program @cmd[] exited with code $exitcode";
        print "Output:\n", $output if $output;
    }
    exit $exitcode;
}
```

There's a big chunk of new features and concepts in here, so let's go through the code bit by bit.

```
sub MAIN(*@cmd) {
```

---

[2]https://docs.raku.org/routine/run
[3]https://docs.raku.org/type/Proc::Async

The first thing you should notice is *@cmd. The * *in front* of the variable indicates a slurpy parameter.[4] It is so named because it slurps up any number of arguments. The * is only needed in the parameter declaration.

So *@cmd collects all the command-line arguments in the array variable @cmd, where the first element is the command to be executed and any further elements are arguments passed to this command.

```
my $proc = Proc::Async.new(|@cmd);
```

The next line creates a new Proc::Async instance with the commands passed in but doesn't yet run anything. Proc::Async.new doesn't expect us to pass an array, but it expects us to pass any number of values as arguments. Therefore, we use the | vertical bar[5] before @cmd to *flatten* our array so that we are sending Proc::Async.new multiple values instead of one array value.

For our program, we need to capture all output from $proc; thus, we capture the output of the STDOUT and STDERR streams (file handles 1 and 2 on Linux) and combine it into a single string. In the asynchronous API, STDOUT and STDERR are modeled as objects of type Supply[6] and hence are streams of events. Since supplies can emit events in parallel, we need a thread-safe data structure for collecting the result, and Raku conveniently provides a Channel for that:

```
my $collector = Channel.new;
```

To actually get the output from the program, we need to tap into the STDOUT and STDERR streams:

```
for $proc.stdout, $proc.stderr -> $supply {
    $supply.tap: { $collector.send($_) }
}
```

---

[4]https://docs.raku.org/type/Signature#Slurpy_ (A.K.A._variadic)_parameters
[5]https://docs.raku.org/type/Signature#index-entry-parameter_|-Capture_ parameters
[6]https://docs.raku.org/type/Supply

Each $supply executes the block { $collector.send($_) } for each string it receives. The string can be a character, a line, or something larger if the stream is buffered. All we do with it is put the string into the channel $collector via the send method.

Note that the preceding code is equivalent to

```
$proc.stdout.tap: { $collector.send($_) }
$proc.stderr.tap: { $collector.send($_) }
```

When running a simple script, you will often see normal output and error output both printed to the terminal together. Our code is interleaving STDOUT and STDERR output into $collector pretty much the same way.

Now that the streams are tapped and wired to our collector, we can start the program and wait for it to finish:

```
my $result = $proc.start.result;
```

Proc::Async.start executes the external process and returns a Promise.[7] A promise wraps a piece of code that potentially runs on another thread, has a status (Planned, Kept or Broken), and, once it's finished, a result. Accessing the result automatically waits for the wrapped code to finish. Here the code is the one that runs the external program, and the result is an object of type Proc[8] (which happens to be the same as the run() function from the synchronous interface).

After this line, we can be sure that the external command has terminated, and thus no more output will come from $proc.stdout and $proc.stderr. Hence, we can safely close the channel and access all its elements through Channel.list:

```
$collector.close;
my $output = $collector.list.join;
```

---

[7]https://docs.raku.org/type/Promise
[8]https://docs.raku.org/type/Proc

Finally, it's time to check if the external command was successful—by checking its exit code—and to exit the wrapper with the command's exit code:

```
my $exitcode = $result.exitcode;
if $exitcode != 0 {
    say "Program @cmd[] exited with code $exitcode";
    print "Output:\n", $output if $output;
}
exit $exitcode;
```

Inside the output string:

```
say "Program @cmd[] exited with code $exitcode";
```

The variable $exitcode is *interpolated*, that is, its name is replaced with its value at runtime. This happens in double-quoted strings, "...", but not in single-quoted strings, '...'. Only scalar variables are interpolated in "..."; other variables (arrays, hashes, code objects) are only interpolated when they are followed by some kind of bracketing construct. That's why @cmd is followed by [ ], which we call a *Zen slice*. An array or hash index that returns more than one value is generally called a *slice*; for example, @cmd[0, 1] returns the first two values. Leaving the index empty returns the whole array.

Another way to achieve interpolation is to add a method call to the variable that ends in parentheses, so it could have also been written as

```
say "Program @cmd.join(' ') exited with code $exitcode";
```

See the documentation[9] for more in-depth information about "..." interpolation.

---

[9]https://docs.raku.org/language/quoting#Interpolation:_qq

6.2 Implementing Timeouts

The idiomatic way to implement timeouts in Raku is to use the `Promise.anyof` combinator together with a timer:

```
sub MAIN(*@cmd, :$timeout) {
    my $proc = Proc::Async.new(|@cmd);
    my $collector = Channel.new;
    for $proc.stdout, $proc.stderr -> $supply {
        $supply.tap: { $collector.send($_) }
    }
    my $promise = $proc.start;
    my $waitfor = $promise;
    $waitfor = Promise.anyof(Promise.in($timeout), $promise)
        if $timeout;
    await $waitfor;
```

The initialization of `$proc` hasn't changed. But instead of accessing `$proc.start.result`, we store the promise returned from `$proc.start`. If the user specified a timeout, we run this piece of code:

```
$waitfor = Promise.anyof(Promise.in($timeout), $promise)
```

`Promise.in($seconds)` returns a promise that will be fulfilled in `$seconds` seconds. It's basically the same as `start { sleep $seconds }`, but the scheduler can be a bit smarter about not allocating a whole thread just for sleeping.

`Promise.anyof($p1, $p2)` returns a promise that is fulfilled as soon as one of the arguments (which should also be promises) is fulfilled. So we wait either until the external program finishes or until the sleep promise is fulfilled.

With `await $waitfor;` the program waits for the promise to be fulfilled (or broken). When that is the case, we can't simply access `$promise.result` as before, because `$promise` (which is the promise for the external program) might not be fulfilled in the case of a timeout. So we have to check the status of the promise first and only then can we safely access $promise.result:

```
if !$timeout || $promise.status ~~ Kept {
    my $exitcode = $promise.result.exitcode;
    $collector.close;
    my $output = $collector.list.join;

    if $exitcode != 0 {
        say "Program @cmd[] exited with code $exitcode";
        print "Output:\n", $output if $output;
    }
    exit $exitcode;
}
else {
    ...
}
```

The expression $promise.status ~~ Kept uses the ~~ *smart matching* operator to check if the promise status is that of the constant Kept. Smart matching is a pretty generic operator, and the semantics depend on the right-hand side of the expression. For a number on the right-hand side, the comparison is a numerical one. For types on the right-hand side, it's a type check. Refer to the official documentation[10] for more.

In the else { ... } branch, we need to handle the timeout case. This might be as simple as printing a statement that a timeout has occurred, and when silent-cron exits immediately afterward, that might be acceptable. But we might want to do more in the future, so we should kill the external program. And if the program doesn't terminate after the friendly kill signal, it should receive a kill(9), which on UNIX systems forcefully terminates the program:

---

[10]https://docs.raku.org/language/operators#infix_~~

```
else {
    $proc.kill;
    say "Program @cmd[] did not finish after $timeout seconds";
    sleep 1 if $promise.status ~~ Planned;
    $proc.kill(9);
    exit 2;
}
```

6.3 More on Promises

If you have worked with concurrent or parallel programs in other languages, you might have come across threads, locks, mutexes, and other low-level constructs. These exist in Raku too, but their direct usage is discouraged.

The problem with such low-level primitives is that they don't compose well. You can have two libraries that use threads and work fine on their own but lead to deadlocks when combined within the same program. Or different components might launch threads on their own, which can lead to too many threads and high memory consumption when several such components come together in the same process.

Raku provides higher-level primitives. Instead of spawning a thread, you use start to run code asynchronously, and the scheduler decides which thread to run this on. If more start calls happen that ask for threads to schedule things on, some will run serially.

Here is a very simple example of running a computation in the background:

```
sub count-primes(Int $upto) {
    (1..$upto).grep(&is-prime).elems;
}
```

```
my $p = start count-primes 10_000;
say $p.status;
await $p;
say $p.result;
```

It gives this output:

```
Planned
1229
```

You can see that the main line of execution continued after the start call and $p immediately had a value—the promise, with status Planned.

As we've seen before, there are combinators for promises, anyof, and allof. You can also chain actions to a promise using the then method:

```
sub count-primes(Int $upto) {
    (1..$upto).grep(&is-prime).elems;
}

my $p1 = start count-primes 10_000;
my $p2 = $p1.then({ say .result });
await $p2;
```

If an exception is thrown inside asynchronously executing code, the status of the promise becomes Broken, and calling its .result method rethrows the exception.

To demonstrate the scheduler distributing tasks, let's consider a small Monte Carlo simulation to calculate an approximation for π. A Monte Carlo simulation is just a program that uses random numbers to explore a space of possible values and comes to a deterministic output (Figure 6-1).

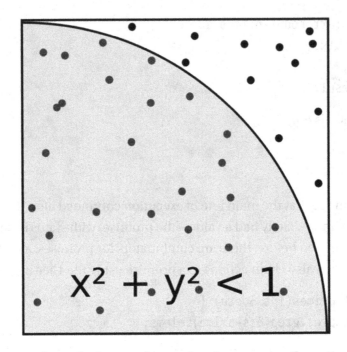

Figure 6-1. *When placing random points in a square, the ratio of points inside a quarter circle to the total number of points approaches π /4*

We generate a pair of random numbers between zero and one and interpret them as dots in a square. A quarter circle with radius one covers the area of π/4, so the ratio of randomly placed dots within the quarter circle to the total number of dots approaches π/4, if we use enough dots.

```
sub pi-approx($iterations) {
    my $inside = 0;
    for 1..$iterations {
        my $x = 1.rand;
        my $y = 1.rand;
        $inside++ if $x * $x + $y * $y <= 1;
    }
    return ($inside / $iterations) * 4;
}
```

```
my @approximations = (1..1000).map({ start pi-approx(80) });
await @approximations;

say @approximations.map({.result}).sum / @approximations;
```

The program starts 1000 computations asynchronously, but if you look at a system monitoring tool while it runs, you'll observe only 16 threads running. This magic number comes from the default thread scheduler, and we can override it by providing our own instance of a scheduler above the previous code:

```
my $*SCHEDULER = ThreadPoolScheduler.new(:max_threads(3));
```

For CPU-bound tasks like this Monte Carlo simulation, it is a good idea to limit the number of threads roughly to the number of (possibly virtual) CPU cores; if many threads are stuck waiting for I/O, a higher number of threads can yield better performance.

6.4 Possible Extensions

If you want to play with silent-cron, you could add a retry mechanism. If a command fails because of an external dependency (like an API or an NFS share), it might take time for that external dependency to recover. Hence, you should add a quadratic or exponential backoff; that is, the wait time between retries should increase quadratically (1, 2, 4, 9, 16, ...) or exponentially (1, 2, 4, 8, 16, 32, ...).

6.5 Refactoring and Automated Tests

Before we extend silent-cron a bit more in the next chapter, it's time to refactor it a bit and write some tests for it.

6.5.1 Refactoring

As a short reminder, this is what the program looks like:

```
#!/usr/bin/env perl6
sub MAIN(*@cmd, :$timeout) {
    my $proc = Proc::Async.new(|@cmd);
    my $collector = Channel.new;
    for $proc.stdout, $proc.stderr -> $supply {
        $supply.tap: { $collector.send($_) }
    }
    my $promise = $proc.start;
    my $waitfor = $promise;
    $waitfor = Promise.anyof(Promise.in($timeout), $promise)
        if $timeout;
    await $waitfor;

    $collector.close;
    my $output = $collector.list.join;

    if !$timeout || $promise.status ~~ Kept {
        my $exitcode = $promise.result.exitcode;
        if $exitcode != 0 {
            say "Program @cmd[] exited with code $exitcode";
            print "Output:\n", $output if $output;
        }
        exit $exitcode;
    }
    else {
        $proc.kill;
        say "Program @cmd[] did not finish after $timeout seconds";
        sleep 1 if $promise.status ~~ Planned;
```

```
    $proc.kill(9);
    exit 2;
  }
}
```

There's logic in there for executing external programs with a timeout as well as logic for dealing with two possible outcomes. In terms of both testability and for future extensions it makes sense to factor out the execution of external programs into a subroutine. The result of this code is not a single value; we're potentially interested in the output it produced, the exit code, and whether it ran into a timeout.

We could write a subroutine that returns a list or a hash of these values, but here I chose to write a small class instead, which the new subroutine will return:

```
class ExecutionResult {
    has Int $.exitcode = -1;
    has Str $.output is required;
    has Bool $.timed-out = False;
    method is-success {
        !$.timed-out && $.exitcode == 0;
    }
}
```

We've seen classes before, but this one has a few new features. Attributes declared with the . twigil automatically get an accessor method, so

```
has Int $.exitcode;
```

is roughly the same as

```
has Int $!exitcode;
method exitcode() { $!exitcode }
```

It allows a user of the class to access the value in the attribute from the outside. As a bonus, you can also initialize it from the standard constructor as a named argument, ExecutionResult.new(exitcode => 42). The exit code is not a required attribute, because we can't know the exit code of a program that has timed out. So with has Int $.exitcode = -1 we give it a default value that applies if the attribute hasn't been initialized.

The output *is* a required attribute, so we mark it as such with is required. That's a *trait*. Traits are pieces of code that modify the behavior of other things, here of an attribute. They crop up in several places, for example, in subroutine signatures (is copy on a parameter), variable declarations, and classes. If you try to call ExecutionResult.new() without specifying an output, you get an error like this:

```
The attribute '$!output' is required, but you did not provide a
value for it.
```

6.5.2 Mocking and Testing

Now that we have a convenient way to return more than one value from a hypothetical subroutine, let's look at what this subroutine might look like:

```
sub run-with-timeout(@cmd, :$timeout) {
    my $proc = Proc::Async.new(|@cmd);
    my $collector = Channel.new;
    for $proc.stdout, $proc.stderr -> $supply {
        $supply.tap: { $collector.send($_) }
    }
    my $promise = $proc.start;
    my $waitfor = $promise;
    $waitfor = Promise.anyof(Promise.in($timeout), $promise)
        if $timeout;
    $ = await $waitfor;
```

```
$collector.close;
my $output = $collector.list.join;

if !$timeout || $promise.status ~~ Kept {
    say "No timeout";
    return ExecutionResult.new(
        :$output,
        :exitcode($promise.result.exitcode),
    );
}
else {
    $proc.kill;
    sleep 1 if $promise.status ~~ Planned;
    $proc.kill(9);
    return ExecutionResult.new(
        :$output,
        :timed-out,
    );
}
}
```

The usage of Proc::Async[11] has remained the same, but instead of producing output when an error occurs, the routine now returns ExecutionResult objects.

This simplifies the MAIN sub quite a bit:

```
multi sub MAIN(*@cmd, :$timeout) {
    my $result = run-with-timeout(@cmd, :$timeout);
    unless $result.is-success {
        say "Program @cmd[] ",
            $result.timed-out ?? "ran into a timeout"
```

---

[11]https://docs.raku.org/type/Proc::Async

```
                        !! "exited with code $result.
                        exitcode()";

    print "Output:\n", $result.output if $result.output;
  }
  exit $result.exitcode // 2;
}
```

A new syntactic feature here is the ternary operator, CONDITION ?? TRUE-BRANCH !! FALSE-BRANCH, which you might know from other programming languages such as C or Perl 5 as CONDITION ? TRUE-BRANCH : FALSE-BRANCH.

Finally, the logical defined-or operator LEFT // RIGHT returns the LEFT side if it's defined and, if not, runs the RIGHT side and returns its value. It works like the || and/or infix operators, except that those check for the boolean value of the left, not whether they are defined.

ℹ   In Raku, we distinguish between defined and true values. By default, all instances are true and defined, and all type objects are false and undefined.

Several built-in types override what they consider to be true. Numbers that equal 0 evaluate to False in a boolean context, as do the empty strings and empty containers such as arrays, hashes, and sets.

On the other hand, only the built-in type Failure[12] overrides definedness.

You can override the truth value of a custom type by implementing a method Bool (which should return True or False) and the definedness with a method defined.

---

[12]https://docs.raku.org/type/Failure

We could start testing the sub `run-with-timeout` by writing custom external commands with defined characteristics (output, runtime, exit code), but that's rather fiddly to do in a reliable, cross-platform way. So instead I want to replace `Proc::Async` with a mock implementation and give the sub a way to inject that:

```
sub run-with-timeout(@cmd, :$timeout, :$executer = Proc::Async)
{
    my $proc = $executer.defined ?? $executer !! $executer.
    new(|@cmd);
    # rest as before
```

Looking through sub `run-with-timeout`, we can make a quick list of methods that the stub `Proc::Async` implementation needs: `stdout`, `stderr`, `start`, and `kill`. Both `stdout` and `stderr` need to return a Supply.[13] The simplest thing that could possibly work is to return a Supply that will emit just a single value:

```
my class Mock::Proc::Async {
    has $.out = '';
    has $.err = '';
    method stdout {
        Supply.from-list($.out);
    }
    method stderr {
        Supply.from-list($.err);
    }
}
```

Supply.from-list[14] returns a Supply that will emit all the arguments passed to it; so here just a single string.

---

[13]https://docs.raku.org/type/Supply
[14]https://docs.raku.org/type/Supply#method_from-list

The simplest possible implementation of kill just does nothing:

```
method kill($?) {}
```

$? in a signature is an optional argument ($foo?) without a name.

Only one method remains that needs to be stubbed: start. It's supposed to return a Promise that, after a defined number of seconds, returns a Proc object or a mock thereof. Since the code only calls the exitcode method on it, writing a stub for it is easy:

```
has $.exitcode = 0;
has $.execution-time = 1;
method start {
    Promise.in($.execution-time).then({
        (class {
            has $.exitcode;
        }).new(:$.exitcode);
    });
}
```

Since we don't need the class for the mock Proc anywhere else, we don't even need to give it a name. class { ... } creates an anonymous class, and the .new call on it creates a new object from it.

A Proc with a nonzero exit code throws an exception when evaluated in void context or *sink context* as we call it in Raku. We can emulate this behavior by extending the anonymous class a bit:

```
class {
    has $.exitcode;
    method sink() {
        die "mock Proc used in sink context";
    }
}
```

With all this preparation in place, we can finally write some tests:

```
multi sub MAIN('test') {
    use Test;

    my class Mock::Proc::Async {
        has $.exitcode = 0;
        has $.execution-time = 0;
        has $.out = '';
        has $.err = '';
        method kill($?) {}
        method stdout {
            Supply.from-list($.out);
        }
        method stderr {
            Supply.from-list($.err);
        }
        method start {
            Promise.in($.execution-time).then({
                (class {
                    has $.exitcode;
                    method sink() {
                        die "mock Proc used in sink context";
                    }
                }).new(:$.exitcode);
            });
        }
    }

    # no timeout, success
    my $result = run-with-timeout([],
        timeout => 2,
        executer => Mock::Proc::Async.new(
```

```
            out => 'mocked output',
        ),
    );
    isa-ok $result, ExecutionResult;
    is $result.exitcode, 0, 'exit code';
    is $result.output, 'mocked output', 'output';
    ok $result.is-success, 'success';

    # timeout
    $result = run-with-timeout([],
        timeout => 0.1,
        executer => Mock::Proc::Async.new(
            execution-time => 1,
            out => 'mocked output',
        ),
    );
    isa-ok $result, ExecutionResult;
    is $result.output, 'mocked output', 'output';
    ok $result.timed-out, 'timeout reported';
    nok $result.is-success, 'success';
}
```

This runs through two scenarios, one where a timeout is configured but not used (because the mocked external program exits first) and one where the timeout takes effect.

6.5.3 Improving Reliability and Timing

Relying on timing in tests is always unattractive. If the times are too short (or too slow together), you risk sporadic test failures on slow or heavily loaded machines. If you use more conservative temporal spacing of tests, the tests can become very slow.

There's a module (not distributed with Rakudo) to alleviate this pain: Test::Scheduler[15] provides a thread scheduler with virtualized time, allowing you to write the tests like this:

```
use Test::Scheduler;
my $*SCHEDULER = Test::Scheduler.new;
my $result = start run-with-timeout([],
    timeout => 5,
    executer => Mock::Proc::Async.new(
        execution-time => 2,
        out => 'mocked output',
    ),
);
$*SCHEDULER.advance-by(5);
$result = $result.result;
isa-ok $result, ExecutionResult;
# more tests here
```

This installs a custom scheduler, and $*SCHEDULER.advance-by(5) instructs it to advance the virtual time by 5 seconds, without having to wait 5 actual seconds. At the time of writing (March 2020), Test::Scheduler has a bug that prevents the second test case from working this way.[16]

6.5.4 Installing a Module

If you want to try out Test::Scheduler, you need to install it first. If you run Rakudo Star, it has already provided you with the zef module installer. You can use that to download and install the module for you:

```
$ zef install Test::Scheduler
```

---

[15]https://github.com/jnthn/p6-test-scheduler
[16]https://github.com/jnthn/p6-test-scheduler/issues/1

If you don't have zef available, you can download, bootstrap, and use it:

```
$ git clone https://github.com/ugexe/zef.git
$ cd zef
$ raku -Ilib bin/zef install.
$ zef install Test::Scheduler
```

6.6 Summary

We've seen an asynchronous API for running external programs and how to use Promises to implement timeouts. We've also discussed how promises are distributed to threads by a scheduler, allowing you to start an arbitrary number of promises without overloading your computer.

During testing, we've seen attributes with accessors, the ternary operator and anonymous classes. Testing of threaded code has been discussed, as has the way in which a third-party module can help. Finally, we had a very small glimpse at the module installer zef.

## CHAPTER 7

Stateful Silent-Cron

In the last chapter, we looked at silent-cron, a wrapper around external programs that silences them in case their exit status is zero. But to make it really practical, it should also silence occasional failures.

External APIs fail, networks become congested, and other things happen that prevent a job from succeeding, so some kind of retry mechanism is desirable. In case of a cron job, cron already takes care of retrying a job on a regular basis, so silent-cron should just suppress occasional errors. On the other hand, if a job fails consistently, this is usually something that an admin or developer should look into, so it's a problem worth reporting.

To implement this functionality, silent-cron needs to store persistent state between separate runs. It needs to record the results from the current run and then decide if the failure history qualifies as "occasional."

We will learn how to use a relational database with Raku.

7.1 Persistent Storage

The storage back end needs to write and retrieve structured data and protect concurrent access to the state file with locking. A good library for such a storage back end is SQLite,[1] a zero-maintenance SQL engine that's

---

[1] www.sqlite.org/

© Moritz Lenz 2020
M. Lenz, *Raku Fundamentals*, https://doi.org/10.1007/978-1-4842-6109-5_7

available as a C library. It's public domain software and in use in most major browsers, operating systems, and even some airliners.[2]

Raku gives you access to SQLite's functionality through DBIish,[3] a generic database interface with back-end drivers for SQLite, MySQL, PostgreSQL, and Oracle DB. To use it, first make sure that SQLite3 is installed, including its header files. On a Debian-based Linux system, for example, you can achieve this with `apt-get install libsqlite3-dev`. If you are using the Rakudo Star distribution, DBIish is already available. If not, you can use one of the module installers to retrieve and install it: `zef install DBIish`.

To use the DBIish's SQLite back end, you first have to create a *database handle* by selecting the back end and supplying connection information:

```
use DBIish;
my $dbh = DBIish.connect('SQLite', :database('database-file.
sqlite3'));
```

Connecting to a SQLite database file that does not yet exist creates that file.

One-off SQL statements can be executed directly on the database handle:

```
$dbh.do('INSERT INTO player (name) VALUES (?)', 'John');
```

The ? in the SQL is a placeholder that is passed out of band as a separate argument to the do method, which avoids potential errors such as SQL injection vulnerabilities.

Queries tend to work by first preparing a statement which returns a *statement handle.* You can execute a statement once or multiple times and retrieve result rows after each `execute` call:

---

[2]`www.sqlite.org/famous.html`
[3]`https://github.com/raku/DBIish/`

```
my $sth = $dbh.prepare('SELECT id FROM player WHERE name = ?');

my %ids;
for <John Jack> -> $name {
    $sth.execute($name);
    %ids{ $name } = $sth.row[0];
}
$sth.finish;
```

7.2 Developing the Storage Back End

We shouldn't just stuff all the storage-handling code into sub MAIN; we should instead carefully consider the creation of a useful API for the storage back end. At first, we need only two pieces of functionality: insert the result of a job execution, and retrieve the most recent results.

Since silent-cron can be used to guard multiple cron jobs on the same machine, we might need something to distinguish the different jobs so that one of them succeeding doesn't prevent error reporting for one that is constantly failing. For that, we introduce a *job name*, which can default to the command (including arguments) being executed but which can be set explicitly on the command line.

The API for the storage back end could look something like this:

```
my $repo = ExecutionResultRepository.new(
    jobname => 'refresh cache',
    statefile => 'silent-cron.sqlite3',
);
$repo.insert($result);
my @last-results = $repo.tail(5);
```

This API isn't specific to the SQLite back end at all; a storage back end that works with plain text files could have the exact same API.

Let's implement this API. First, we need the class and the two attributes that should be obvious from the preceding usage example:

```
class ExecutionResultRepository {
    has $.jobname    is required;
    has $.statefile is required;
    # ... more code
```

To implement the insert method, we need to connect to the database and create the relevant table if it doesn't exist yet.

```
has $!db;
method !db() {
    return $!db if $!db;
    $!db = DBIish.connect('SQLite', :database($.statefile));
    self!create-schema();
    return $!db;
}
```

This code uses a private attribute $!db to cache the database handle and a private method !db to create the handle if it doesn't exist yet.

Private methods are declared like ordinary methods, except that the name starts with an exclamation mark. To call one, substitute the method call dot for the exclamation mark; in other words, use self!db() instead of self.db().

The !db method also calls the next private method, !create-schema, which creates the storage table and some indexes:

```
constant $table = 'job_execution';
method !create-schema() {
    $!db.do(qq:to/SCHEMA/);
        CREATE TABLE IF NOT EXISTS $table (
            id          INTEGER PRIMARY KEY,
            jobname     VARCHAR NOT NULL,
```

```
        exitcode    INTEGER NOT NULL,
        timed_out   INTEGER NOT NULL,
        output      VARCHAR NOT NULL,
        executed    TIMESTAMP NOT NULL DEFAULT
                    (DATETIME('NOW'))
    );
SCHEMA
$!db.do(qq:to/INDEX/);
    CREATE INDEX IF NOT EXISTS {$table}_jobname_exitcode ON
    $table ( jobname, exitcode );
INDEX
$!db.do(qq:to/INDEX/);
    CREATE INDEX IF NOT EXISTS {$table}_jobname_executed ON
    $table ( jobname, executed );
INDEX
}
```

Multiline string literals are best written with the *heredoc*[4] syntax.
qq:to/DELIMITER/ tells Raku to finish parsing the current line so that you
can still close the method call parenthesis and add the statement-ending
semicolon. The next line starts the string literal, which goes on until
the parser finds the delimiter on a line on its own. Leading whitespace
is stripped from each line of the string literal by as much as the closing
delimiter is indented.

Thus,

```
print q:to/EOS/;
    Not indented
        Indented four spaces
    EOS
```

---

[4]https://docs.raku.org/language/quoting#Heredocs:_:to

produces the output

```
Not indented
    Indented four spaces
```

Now that we have a working database connection and know that the database table exists, inserting a new record becomes easy:

```
method insert(ExecutionResult $r) {
    self!db.do(qq:to/INSERT/, $.jobname, $r.exitcode, $r.timed-
    out, $r.output);
        INSERT INTO $table (jobname, exitcode, timed_out,
        output)
        VALUES(?, ?, ?, ?)
    INSERT
}
```

Selecting the most recent records is a bit more work, partially because we need to convert the table rows into objects:

```
method tail(Int $count) {
    my $sth = self!db.prepare(qq:to/SELECT/);
        SELECT exitcode, timed_out, output
          FROM $table
         WHERE jobname = ?
      ORDER BY executed DESC
         LIMIT $count
    SELECT
    $sth.execute($.jobname);
    $sth.allrows(:array-of-hash).map: -> %h {
        ExecutionResult.new(
            exitcode  => %h<exitcode>,
            timed-out => ?%h<timed_out>,
```

```
        output    => %h<output>,
    );
  }
}
```

The last statement in the `tail` method deserves a bit of extra attention. `$sth.allrows(:array- of-hash)` produces the database rows as a list of hashes. This list is *lazy*, that is, it's generated on demand. Lazy lists are a very convenient feature because they allow you to use iterators and lists with the same API. For instance, when reading lines from a file, you can write `for $handle.lines -> $line { ... }`, and the `lines` method doesn't have to load the whole file into memory; instead it can read a line whenever it is accessed.

`$sth.allrows(...)` is lazy, and so is the `.map` call that comes after it. `map` transforms a list one element at a time by calling the code object that's passed to it. And that is done lazily as well. So SQLite only retrieves rows from the database file when elements of the resulting list are actually accessed.

7.3 Using the Storage Back End

With the storage API in place, it's time to use it:

```
multi sub MAIN(*@cmd, :$timeout, :$jobname is copy,
               :$statefile='silent-cron.sqlite3',
               Int :$tries = 3) {
    $jobname //= @cmd.Str;
    my $result = run-with-timeout(@cmd, :$timeout);
    my $repo = ExecutionResultRepository.new(:$jobname,
    :$statefile);
    $repo.insert($result);

    my @runs = $repo.tail($tries);
```

```
unless $result.is-success or @runs.grep({.is-success}) {
    say "The last @runs.elems() runs of @cmd[] all failed,
    the last execution ",
        $result.timed-out ?? "ran into a timeout"
                          !! "exited with code $result.
                          exitcode()";

    print "Output:\n", $result.output if $result.output;
}
exit $result.exitcode // 2;
}
```

Now, a job that succeeds a few times and then fails up to two times in a row doesn't produce any error output; only the third failed execution in a row produces output. You can override that on the command line with `--tries=5`.

The `MAIN` subroutine uses the construct `$var //= EXPR`. The `//` stands for *defined-OR*, so it returns the left-hand side if it has a defined value. Otherwise, it evaluates and returns the value of `EXPR`. Combined with the assignment operator, it evaluates the right-hand side only if the variable is undefined and then stores the value of the expression in the variable. This is a handy way to ensure that a variable gets a value or even a short way to write a cache.

7.4 Room for Expansion

A system administrator who has to investigate why a cron job failed might be interested in a history of that job. You could implement a command that lists the last job runs, their success or failure, their exit code, or possibly their runtime, and so on.

In addition, in regular operation you'd need some code to automatically delete old job entries, to prevent the state database from growing indefinitely.

Or you could investigate a different back end. What if you wanted to store the state in JSON files instead of SQLite? Or enable both? (Hint: You could use the JSON::Tiny[5] or JSON::Fast[6] modules.)

7.5 Summary

We've discussed DBIish, a database API with a pluggable back end, and explored using it with SQLite to store persistent data. In the process, we also came across lazy lists and a new form of string literals called *heredocs*.

---

[5]https://github.com/moritz/json
[6]https://github.com/timo/json_fast

CHAPTER 8

Review of the Raku Basics

In the previous chapters, we discussed some examples interleaved with the Raku mechanics that make them work. Here I want to summarize and deepen the Raku knowledge that we've touched on so far, removed from the original examples.

8.1 Variables and Scoping

In Raku, variable names are made of a *sigil*, $, @, %, or &, followed by an identifier. The sigil implies a type constraint, where $ is the most general one (no restriction by default), @ is for arrays, % is for hashes (associative arrays/maps), and & is for code objects.

Identifiers can contain - and ' characters, as long as the character after it is a letter. Identifiers must start with a letter or underscore.

Subroutines and variables declared with my are lexically scoped. They are visible from the point of the declaration to the end of the current {}-enclosed block (or the current file, in case the declaration is outside a block). Subroutine parameters are visible in the signature and block of the subroutine.

An optional *twigil* between the sigil and identifier can influence the scoping. The * twigil marks a dynamically scoped variable; thus, lookup is performed in the current call stack. ! marks attributes, that is, a per-instance variable that's attached to an object.

© Moritz Lenz 2020
M. Lenz, *Raku Fundamentals*, https://doi.org/10.1007/978-1-4842-6109-5_8

8.2 Subroutines

A subroutine, or *sub for short*, is a piece of code with its own scope and usually also a name. It has a *signature* that specifies what kind of values you have to pass in when you call it:

```
sub chunks(Str $s, Int $chars) {
#         ^^^^^^^^^^^^^^^^^^^^ signature
#   ^^^^^^ name
    gather for 0 .. $s.chars / $chars - 1 -> $idx {
        take substr($s, $idx * $chars, $chars);
    }
}
```

The variables used in the signature are called *parameters*, whereas we call the values that you pass in *arguments*.

To refer to a subroutine without calling it, put an ampersand (&) in front of it, like so:

```
say &chunks.name;       # Output: chunks
```

To call it, simply use its name, followed by the list of arguments, which can optionally be in parentheses:

```
say chunks 'abcd', 2;   # Output: (ab cd)
say chunks('abcd', 2);  # Output: (ab cd)
```

You only need the parentheses if some other construct would otherwise interfere with the subroutine call. Hence, if you intend to write

```
say chunks(join('x', 'ab', 'c'), 2);
```

and you leave out the inner pair of parentheses

```
say chunks(join 'x', 'ab', 'c', 2);
```

then all the arguments go to the join function, leaving only one argument to the chunks function. On the other hand, it is fine to omit the outer pair of parentheses and write

```
say chunks join('x', 'ab', 'c'), 2;
```

because there's no ambiguity here.

One case worth noting is that if you call a subroutine without arguments as the block of an if condition or a for loop (or similar constructs), you have to include the parentheses, because otherwise the block is parsed as an argument to the function.

```
sub random-choice() {
    Bool.pick;
}

# right way:
if random-choice() {
    say 'You were lucky.';
}

# wrong way:
if random-choice {
    say 'You were lucky.';
}
```

If you do happen to make this mistake, the Raku compiler tries very hard to detect it. In the preceding example, it says

```
Function 'random-choice' needs parens to avoid gobbling block
```

and when it tries to parse the block for the if statement, it doesn't find one:

```
Missing block (apparently claimed by 'random-choice')
```

When you have a sub called MAIN, Raku uses its signature to parse the command-line arguments and pass those command-line arguments to MAIN.

multi subs are several subroutines with the same name but different signatures. The compiler decides at runtime which of the candidates it calls based on the best match between arguments and parameters.

8.3 Classes and Objects

Class declarations follow the same syntactic schema as subroutine declarations: the keyword class, followed by the name, followed by the body in curly braces:

```
class OutputCapture {
    has @!lines;
    method print(\s) {
        @!lines.push(s);
    }
    method captured() {
        @!lines.join;
    }
}
```

By default, type names are scoped to the current namespace; however, you can make it lexically scoped by adding a my in front of class:

```
my class OutputCapture { ... }
```

Creating a new instance generally works by calling the new method on the type object. The new method is inherited from the implicit parent class Any that all types get:

```
my $c = OutputCapture.new;
```

Per-instance state is stored in *attributes*, which are declared with the has keyword, as seen in the preceding has @!lines. Attributes are always private, as indicated by the ! twigil. If you use the dot . twigil in the declaration instead, you have both the private attribute @!lines and a public, read-only accessor method:

```
my class OutputCapture {
    has @.lines;
    method print(\s) {
        # the private name with ! still works
        @!lines.push(s);
    }
    method captured() {
        @!lines.join;
    }
}
my $c = OutputCapture.new;
$c.print('42');
# use the `lines` accessor method:
say $c.lines;        # Output: [42]
```

When you declare attributes with the dot twigil, you can also initialize the attributes from the constructor through named arguments, as in OutputCapture.new(lines => [42]).

Private methods start with a ! and can only be called from inside the class body as self!private-method.

Methods are basically subroutines, with two differences. The first is that they get an implicit parameter called self, which contains the object the method is called on (which we call the *invocant*). The second is that if you call a subroutine, the compiler searches for this subroutine in the current lexical scope as well as the outer scopes. On the other hand, method calls are looked up only in the class of the object and its superclasses.

The subroutine lookup can happen at compile time, because lexical scopes are immutable at runtime, so the compiler has knowledge of all lexical symbols. However, even in the presence of type constraints, the compiler can't know if the type of an object is possibly a subtype of a type constraint, which means method lookups must be deferred to runtime.

8.4 Concurrency

Raku provides high-level primitives for concurrency and parallel execution. Instead of explicitly spawning new threads, you are encouraged to run a computation with start, which returns a Promise.[1] This is an object that promises a future computation will yield a result. The status can thus be Planned, Kept, or Broken. You can chain promises, combine them, and wait for them.

In the background, a scheduler distributes such computations to operating system–level threads. The default scheduler is a thread pool scheduler with an upper limit to the number of threads available for use.

Communication between parallel computations should happen through thread-safe data structures. Foremost among them are Channel[2] (a thread-safe queue) and Supply[3] (Raku's implementation of the Observer Pattern[4]). Supplies are very powerful, because you can transform them with methods such as map, grep, throttle, or delayed and use their actor semantic[5] to ensure that a consumer is run in only one thread at a time.

---

[1]https://docs.raku.org/type/Promise
[2]https://docs.raku.org/type/Channel
[3]https://docs.raku.org/type/Supply
[4]https://en.wikipedia.org/wiki/Observer_pattern
[5]https://docs.raku.org/type/Supply#method_act

8.5 Outlook

When you understand the topics discussed in this chapter, and dig a bit into the built-in types, you should be familiar with the basics of Raku and be able to write your own programs.

Next we will look into one of the strengths of Raku: parsing, via regexes and grammars.

CHAPTER 9

Parsing INI Files Using Regexes and Grammars

You've probably seen .ini files before; they are quite common as configuration files on the Microsoft Windows platform but are also found in many other places such as ODBC configuration files, Ansible's inventory files,[1] and so on.

This is what they look like:

```
key1=value2
```

[section1]
```
key2=value2
key3 = with spaces
; comment lines start with a semicolon, and are
; ignored by the parser
```

[section2]
```
more=stuff
```

---

[1]http://docs.ansible.com/ansible/intro_inventory.html

© Moritz Lenz 2020
M. Lenz, *Raku Fundamentals*, https://doi.org/10.1007/978-1-4842-6109-5_9

Raku offers regexes for parsing and grammars for structuring and reusing regexes.

You could use the Config::INI[2] module (after installing with `zef install Config::INI`) to parse files INI files like so:

```
use Config::INI;
my %hash = Config::INI::parse($ini_string);
```

Under the hood it uses regexes and grammars. Here, we will explore how we could write our own INI parser.

9.1 Regex Basics

A *regex* is a piece of code that acts as a pattern for strings with a common structure. It's derived from the computer science concept of a *regular expression*[3] but adapted to provide more constructs than pure regular expressions allow and extended with some features that make them easier to use.

We'll use named regexes to match the primitives and then use regexes that call these named regexes to build a parser for the INI files. Since INI files have no universally accepted, formal grammar, we have to make stuff up as we go.

Let's start with parsing value pairs, like `key1=value1`. First let's consider just the key. It may contain letters, digits, and the underscore `_`. There's a shortcut to match such characters, `\w`, and matching one or more works by appending a + character:

```
use v6.d;

my regex key { \w+ }
```

---

[2]https://modules.raku.org/dist/Config::INI
[3]https://en.wikipedia.org/wiki/Regular_expression

```
multi sub MAIN('test') {
    use Test;
    ok 'abc'    ~~ /^ <key> $/, '<key> matches a simple identifier';
    ok '[abc]' !~~ /^ <key> $/, '<key> does not match a section
    header';
    done-testing;
}
```

`my regex key { \w+ }` declares a lexically (*my*) scoped regex called key that matches one or more word characters.

There is a long tradition in programming languages to support so-called Perl Compatible Regular Expressions (PCRE). Many programming languages support some deviations from PCRE, including Perl itself, but common syntax elements remain throughout most implementations. Raku still supports some of these elements but deviates substantially in others.

Here `\w+` is the same as in PCRE, but in contrast to PCRE, whitespace in the regex is ignored. This allows you to write much more readable regexes, with freedom to format regexes just like you would with normal code.

In the testing routine, the slashes in `'abc' ~~ /^ <key> $/` delimit an anonymous regex. In this regex, `^` and `$` stand for the start and the end of the matched string, respectively, which is familiar from PCRE. However, in contrast to PCRE, the `<key>` subrule calls the named regex key from earlier. This is a Raku extension. In PCRE, the `<` in a regex matches a literal `<`. In Raku regexes, it introduces a subrule call.

In general, all nonword characters are reserved for "special" syntax, and you have to quote or backslash them to get the literal meaning. For example, `\<` or `'<'` in a regex matches a less than sign. Quoting can apply to more than one character, so `'a+b'` in a regex matches an a, followed by a plus +, followed by a b.

Word characters (letters, digits, and the underscore) always match literally.

9.1.1 Character Classes

Besides literals, character classes are a common building block of regexes. There are many predefined character classes in the form of a backslash followed by a lowercase single letter; for example, \d matches a digit. Its inverse uses the uppercase letter, so \D matches any character that is *not* a digit.

Character Class	Negation	Matches
\d	\D	A digit
\w	\W	A word character (letter, digit, underscore)
\s	\S	Whitespace, blanks, newlines, etc.
\h	\H	Horizontal whitespace
\v	\V	Vertical whitespace
\n	\N	Logical newline (carriage return, line feed)
.		Any character

You can also build your own character classes by enumerating characters or ranges of characters:

Method	Example	Matches
Enumeration	<[abc]>	a, b, or c
Negation	<-[abc]>	Anything except a, b, or c
Range	<[a..c]>	a, b, or c

Let's formulate some of these character classes and their properties as tests, all of which pass:

```
use Test;

ok  'a' ~~ /\w/, '"a" matches \w';
ok  'Σ' ~~ /\w/, 'Greek Sigma matches \w';
nok '!' ~~ /\w/, 'bang ! is not a word character';
nok 'ab' ~~ /^ \w $/, '\w matches just one char';
ok  'b' ~~ /<[abc]>/, 'enumeration';
nok 'B' ~~ /<[abc]>/, 'enumeration is case sensitive';
ok  'a' ~~ /<[a..c]>/, 'in range';
nok 'd' ~~ /<[a..c]>/, 'out of range';

done-testing;
```

The official Raku test suite contains many of such tests[4]; we just have a few here to illustrate the behavior of the character classes.

9.1.2 Quantifiers

Matching only one repetition of anything is boring, so regexes offer *quantifiers*. A quantifier states how often the previous regex must match.

Quantifier	Matches how many characters?
*	0..Inf
+	1..Inf
?	0..1
** 3	3
** 1..5	1..5

[4]See, for example, https://github.com/Raku/roast/blob/master/ S05-metasyntax/charset.t.

Again, some examples in the form of passing tests:

```
nok 'ba'       ~~ / ^ ba [na]+ $ /, '+ must match at least once';
ok  'bana'     ~~ / ^ ba [na]+ $ /, '+ with a single match';
ok  'banana'   ~~ / ^ ba [na]+ $ /, '+ with two matches';
ok  'bananana' ~~ / ^ ba [na]+ $ /, '+ with three matches';
```

9.1.3 Alternatives

Either-or alternatives are separated by the vertical bar |. For example, \d+
| x matches either a sequence of one or more digits or the character x.

If more than one path of an alternative matches, Raku prefers the
longest match. If that behavior is not desired, || takes the first alternative
that matches. Formulated as tests:

```
ok  'a' ~~ /a|b|c/,  'first branch of an alternative';
ok  'c' ~~ /a|b|c/,  'third branch of an alternative';
nok 'd' ~~ /a|b|c/,  'not part of alternative';
is 'x42' ~~ /x | \w+/, 'x42', 'longer branch wins';
is 'x42' ~~ /a||x||\w+/, 'x', 'with || first matching branch
wins';
```

9.2 Parsing the INI Primitives

Coming back to INI parsing, we have to think about what characters are
allowed inside a value. Listing allowed characters seems to be like a futile
exercise, since we are very likely to forget some. Instead, we should think
about what's *not* allowed in a value. Newlines certainly aren't, because
they introduce the next key/value pair or a section heading. Neither are
semicolons allowed, because they introduce a comment.

We can formulate this exclusion as a negated character class: <-[\n ;]> matches any single character that is neither a newline nor a semicolon. Note that inside a character class, nearly all characters lose their special meaning. Only backslash, whitespace, two dots, and the closing bracket stand for anything other than themselves. Inside and outside of character classes alike, \n matches a single newline character and \s whitespace. The uppercase inverts that, so that, for example, \S matches any single character that is not whitespace.

This leads us to a version of a regex to match a value in an INI file:

```
my regex value { <-[ \n ; ]>+ }
```

There is one problem with this regex: it also matches leading and trailing whitespace, which we don't want to consider as part of the value:

```
my regex value { <-[ \n ; ]>+ }
if ' abc ' ~~ /<value>/ {
    say "matched '$/'";              # matched ' abc '
}
```

If Raku regexes were limited to a regular language in the computer science sense, we'd have to do something like this:

```
my regex value {
    # match a first non-whitespace character
    <-[ \s ; ]>
    [
        # then arbitrarily many that can contain whitespace
        <-[ \n ; ]>*
        # ... terminated by one non-whitespace
        <-[ \s ; ]>
    ]? # and make it optional, in case the value is only
       # only one non-whitespace character
}
```

And now you know why people respond with "And now you have *two* problems"[5] when proposing to solve problems with regexes. A simpler solution is to match a value as introduced first and then to introduce a constraint that neither the first nor the last character may be whitespace:

```
my regex value { <!before \s> <-[ \n ; ]>+ <!after \s> }
```

along with accompanying tests:

```
is ' abc ' ~~ /<value>/, 'abc', '<value> does not match leading
or trailing whitespace';
is ' a' ~~ /<value>/, 'a', '<value> matches single non-
whitespace too';
ok "a\nb" !~~ /^ <value> $/, '<value> does not match \n';
```

`<!before regex>` is a negated look-ahead, that is, the following text must not match the regex, and the text isn't consumed while matching. Unsurprisingly, `<!after regex>` is the negated look-behind, which tries to match text that has already been matched and must not succeed in doing so for the whole match to be successful.

This being Raku, there is of course yet another way to approach this problem. If you formulate the requirements as "a value must not contain a newline or semicolon *and* start with a non-whitespace *and* end with a non-whitespace," it becomes obvious that if we just had an AND operator in regexes, this could be easy. And it is

```
my regex value { <-[ \n ; ]>+ & \S.* & .*\S }
```

The & operator delimits two or more smaller regex expressions that must all match the same string successfully for the whole match to succeed. `\S.*` matches any string that starts with a non-whitespace character (`\S`), followed by any character (`.`) any number of times `*`. Likewise, `.*\S` matches any string that ends with a non-whitespace character.

---

[5]http://regex.info/blog/2006-09-15/247

Who would have thought that matching something as seemingly simple as a value in a configuration file could be so involved? Luckily, matching a key/value pair is much simpler now that we know how to match each on their own:

my regex pair { <key> '=' <value> }

And this works great, as long as there are no blanks surrounding the equality sign. If there are, we have to match them separately:

my regex pair { <key> \h* '=' \h* <value> }

\h matches a horizontal whitespace, that is, a blank, a tabulator character, or any other fancy spacelike thing that Unicode has in store for us (e.g., also the nonbreaking space) but not a newline.

Speaking of newlines, it's a good idea to match a newline at the end of regex pair, and since we ignore empty lines, let's match more than one as well:

my regex pair { <key> \h* '=' \h* <value> \n+ }

Time to write some tests:

```
ok "key=value\n" ~~ /<pair>/, 'simple pair';
ok "key = value\n\n" ~~ /<pair>/, 'pair with blanks';
ok "key\n= value\n" !~~ /<pair>/, 'pair with newline before
assignment';
```

A section header is a string in square brackets, so the string itself shouldn't contain brackets or a newline:

my regex header { '[' <-[\[\] \n]>+ ']' \n+ }

```
# and in multi sub MAIN('test'):
ok "[abc]\n"    ~~ /^ <header> $/, 'simple header';
ok "[a c]\n"    ~~ /^ <header> $/, 'header with spaces';
ok "[a [b]]\n" !~~ /^ <header> $/, 'cannot nest headers';
ok "[a\nb]\n"  !~~ /^ <header> $/, 'No newlines inside headers';
```

The last remaining primitive is the comment

```
my regex comment { ';' \N*\n+ }
```

\N matches any character that's not a newline, so the comment is just a semicolon, and then anything until the end of the line.

9.3 Putting Things Together

A *section* of an INI file is a header followed by some key/value pairs or comment lines:

```
my regex section {
    <header>
    [ <pair> | <comment> ]*
}
```

[...] groups a part of a regex so that the quantifier * after it applies to the whole group, not just to the last term.

The whole INI file consists of potentially some initial key/value pairs or comments followed by some sections:

```
my regex inifile {
    [ <pair> | <comment> ]*
    <section>*
}
```

The avid reader has noticed that the [<pair> | <comment>]* part of a regex has been used twice, so it's a good idea to extract it into a stand-alone regex:

```
my regex block   { [ <pair> | <comment> ]* }
my regex section { <header> <block> }
my regex inifile { <block> <section>* }
```

It's time for the "ultimate" test:

```
my $ini = q:to/EOI/;
key1=value2

[section1]
key2=value2
key3 = with spaces
; comment lines start with a semicolon, and are
; ignored by the parser

[section2]
more=stuff
EOI

ok $ini ~~ /^<inifile>$/, 'Can parse a full INI file';
```

9.4 Backtracking

Regex matching seems magical to many programmers. You just state the pattern, and the regex engine determines for you whether a string matches the pattern or not. While implementing a regex engine is a tricky business, the basics aren't too hard to understand.

The regex engine goes through the parts of a regex from left to right, trying to match each part of the regex. It keeps track of what part of the string it matched so far in a *cursor*. If a part of a regex can't find a match, the regex engine tries to alter the previous match to take up fewer characters and then retry the failed match at the new position.

For instance, if you execute the regex match

```
'abc' ~~ /.* b/
```

the regex engine first evaluates the .*. The . matches any character. The * quantifier is *greedy*, which means it tries to match as many characters as it can. It ends up matching the whole string, abc. Then the regex engine tries to match the b, which is a literal. Since the previous match gobbled up the whole string, matching b against the remaining empty string fails. So the previous regex part, .*, must give up a character. It now matches ab, and the literal matcher for the b compares b from the regex against the third character of the string, c, and fails again. So there is a final iteration where the .* once again gives up one character it matched, and now the b literal can match the second character in the string.

This back and forth between the parts of a regex is called *backtracking*. It's a great feature when you search for a pattern in a string. But in a parser, it is usually not desirable. If, for example, the regex key matched the substring key2 in the input key2=value2, you don't want it to match a shorter substring just because the next part of the regex can't match.

There are three major reasons why you don't want that. The first is that it makes debugging harder. When humans think about how a text is structured, they usually commit pretty quickly to basic tokenization, such as where a word or a sentence ends. Thus backtracking can be very unintuitive. If you generate error messages based on which regexes failed to match, backtracking basically always leads to the error message being pretty useless.

The second reason is that backtracking can lead to unexpected regex matches. For example, you want to match two words, optionally separated by whitespace, and you try to translate this directly to a regex:

```
say "two words" ~~ /\w+\s*\w+/;     # 「two words」
```

This seems to work: the first \w+ matches the first word, and the second one matches the second word, all fine and good—until you find that it actually matches a single word too:

```
say "two" ~~ /\w+\s*\w+/;               # 「two」
```

How did that happen? Well, the first \w+ matched the whole word, \s*
successfully matched an empty string due to the * quantifier, and then
the second \w+ failed, forcing the previous two parts of the regex to match
differently. So in the second iteration, the first \w+ only matches tw, the \s*
matches the empty string between tw and o, and the second \w+ matches
o. And then you realize that if two words aren't delimited by whitespace,
how do you even tell where one word ends and the next one starts? With
backtracking disabled, the regex fails to match instead of matching in an
unintended way.

The third reason is performance. When you disable backtracking,
the regex engine has to look at each character only once or once for each
branch it can take in the case of alternatives. With backtracking, the regex
engine can be stuck in backtracking loops that take overproportionally
longer with increasing length of the input string.

To disable backtracking, you simply have to replace the word regex
by token in the declaration or by using the :ratchet modifier inside the
regex.

In the INI file parser, only the regex value needs backtracking (though
other formulations discussed in the preceding don't need it); all the other
regexes can be switched over to tokens safely:

```
my token key     { \w+ }
my regex value   { <!before \s> <-[\n;]>+ <!after \s> }
my token pair    { <key> \h* '=' \h* <value> \n+ }
my token header  { '[' <-[ \[ \] \n ]>+ ']' \n+ }
my token comment { ';' \N*\n+  }
my token block { [ <pair> | <comment> ]* }
my token section { <header> <block> }
my token inifile { <block> <section>* }
```

9.5 Grammars

This collection of regexes that parse INI files is not the pinnacle of encapsulation and reusability.

Hence, we'll explore grammars, a feature that groups regexes into a class-like structure, and how to extract structured data from a successful match.

A *grammar* is a class with some extra features that make it suitable for parsing text. Along with methods and attributes, you can put regexes into a grammar.

This is what the INI file parser looks like when formulated as a grammar:

```
grammar IniFile {
    token key     { \w+ }
    regex value   { <!before \s> <-[\n;]>+ <!after \s> }
    token pair    { <key> \h* '=' \h* <value> \n+ }
    token header  { '[' <-[ \[ \] \n ]>+ ']' \n+ }
    token comment { ';' \N*\n+   }
    token block   { [<pair> | <comment>]* }
    token section { <header> <block> }
    token TOP     { <block> <section>* }
}
```

You can use it to parse some text by calling the `parse` method, which uses regex or token TOP as the entry point:

```
my $result = IniFile.parse($text);
```

Besides the standardized entry point, a grammar offers more advantages. You can inherit from it like from a normal class, thus bringing even more reusability to regexes. You can group extra functionality together with the regexes by adding methods to the grammar. There are also some mechanisms in grammars that can make your life as a developer easier.

One of them is dealing with whitespace. In INI files, horizontal whitespace is generally considered to be insignificant, in that key=value and key = value lead to the same configuration of the application. So far we've dealt with that explicitly by adding \h* to token pair. But there are places we haven't actually considered. For example, it's OK to have a comment that's not at the start of the line.

The mechanism that grammars offer is that you can define a regex called ws[6], and when you declare a token with rule instead of token (or enable this feature in regex through the :sigspace modifier), Raku inserts implicit <ws> calls for you where there is whitespace in the regex definition:

```
grammar IniFile {
    token ws { \h* }
    rule pair { <key>     '='     <value> \n+ }
    # rest as before
}
```

This might not be worth the effort for a single rule that needs to parse whitespace, but when there are more, this really pays off by keeping whitespace parsing in a single location.

Note that you should only parse insignificant whitespace in token ws. In the case of INI files, newlines are significant, so we shouldn't match them.

9.6 Extracting Data from the Match

So far the IniFile grammar only checks whether a given input matches the grammar or not. However, when it does match, we really want the parse result in a data structure that's easy to use. For instance, we could translate this example INI file:

---

[6]https://docs.raku.org/language/grammars#ws

```
key1=value2

[section1]
key2=value2
key3 = with spaces
; comment lines start with a semicolon and are
; ignored by the parser

[section2]
more=stuff
```

into this data structure of nested hashes:

```
{
    _ => {
        key1 => "value2"
    },
    section1 => {
        key2 => "value2",
        key3 => "with spaces"
    },
    section2 => {
        more => "stuff"
    }
}
```

Note that key/value pairs from outside any section show up in the _ top-level key.

The result from the IniFile.parse call is a Match[7] object that has (nearly) all the information necessary to extract the desired match. If you turn a Match object into a string, it becomes the matched string.

---

[7]https://docs.raku.org/type/Match

But there's more. You can use it like a hash to extract the matches from named submatches. Hence, if the top-level match from

token TOP { <block> <section>* }

produces a Match object $m, then $m<block> is again a Match object, this one from the match of the call of token block. And $m<section> is a list of Match objects from the repeated calls to token section. So a Match is really a tree of matches (Figure 9-1).

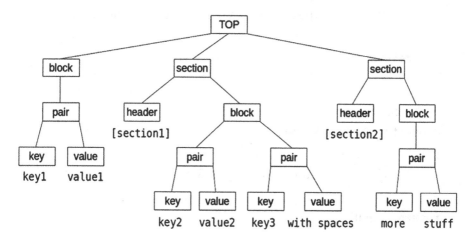

Figure 9-1. *Match tree from parsing the example INI file*

We can walk this data structure to extract the nested hashes. The header token matches a string like "[section1]\n", and we're only interested in "section1". To get to the inner part, we can modify header by inserting a pair of parentheses around the subregex whose match we're interested in:

token header { '[' (<-[\[\] \n]>+) ']' \n+ }
^^^^^^^^^^^^^^^^^^^^^^ *a capturing group*

That's a *capturing group*, and we can get its match by using the top-level match for header as an array and access its first element. This leads us to the full INI parser:

115

```
sub parse-ini(Str $input) {
    my $m = IniFile.parse($input);
    unless $m {
        die "The input is not a valid INI file.";
    }

    sub block(Match $m) {
        my %result;
        for $m<block><pair> -> $pair {
            %result{ $pair<key>.Str } = $pair<value>.Str;
        }
        return %result;
    }

    my %result;
    %result<_> = block($m);
    for $m<section> -> $section {
        %result{ $section<header>[0].Str } = block($section);
    }
    return %result;
}
```

This top-down approach works, but it requires a very intimate understanding of the grammar's structure. This means that if you change the structure during maintenance, you'll have a hard time figuring out how to change the data extraction code.

Raku offers a bottom-up approach as well. It allows you to write a data extraction or *action* method for each regex, token, or rule. The grammar engine passes in the match object as the single argument, and the action method can call the routine make to attach a result to the match object. The result is available through the .made method on the match object.

This execution of action methods happens as soon as a regex matches successfully; thus, an action method for a regex can rely on the fact that the action methods for subregex calls have already run. For example, when the rule pair { <key> '=' <value> \n+ } is being executed, first token key matches successfully, and its action method runs immediately. Then, token value matches, and its action method runs too. Finally, the rule pair itself can match successfully, so its action method can rely on $m<key>. made and $m<value>.made being available, assuming that the match result is stored in variable $m.

Speaking of variables, a regex match implicitly stores its result in the special variable $/, and it is customary to use $/ as a parameter in action methods. There is also a shortcut for accessing named submatches: instead of writing $/<key>, you can write $<key>. With this convention in mind, the action class becomes

```
class IniFile::Actions {
    method key($/)     { make $/.Str }
    method value($/)   { make $/.Str }
    method header($/)  { make $/[0].Str }
    method pair($/)    { make $<key>.made => $<value>.made }
    method block($/)   { make $<pair>.map({ .made }).hash }
    method section($/) { make $<header>.made => $<block>.made }
    method TOP($/)     {
        make {
            _ => $<block>.made,
            $<section>.map: { .made },
        }
    }
}
```

The first two action methods are really simple. The result of a key or value match is simply the string that matched. For a header, it's just the substring inside the brackets. Fittingly, a pair returns a Pair[8] object, composed from key and value. The block method constructs a hash

---

[8]https://docs.raku.org/type/Pair

from all the lines in the block by iterating over each `pair` submatch and extracting the already attached `Pair` object. One level above that in the match tree `section` takes that hash and pairs it with the name of section, extracted from `$<header>.made`. Finally, the top-level action method gathers the sectionless key/value pairs under the key `_` as well as all the sections and returns them in a hash.

In each method of the action class, we only rely on the knowledge of the first level of regexes called directly from the regex that corresponds to the action method and the data types that they `.made`. Thus, when you refactor one regex, you also have to change only the corresponding action method. Nobody needs to be aware of the global structure of the grammar.

Now we just have to tell Raku to actually use the action class:

```
sub parse-ini(Str $input) {
    my $m = IniFile.parse($input, :actions(IniFile::Actions));
    unless $m {
        die "The input is not a valid INI file.";
    }

    return $m.made
}
```

If you want to start parsing with a different rule than TOP (e.g., which you might want to do in a test), you can pass a named argument `rule` to method `parse`:

```
sub parse-ini(Str $input, :$rule = 'TOP') {
    my $m = IniFile.parse($input,
        :actions(IniFile::Actions),
        :$rule,
    );
    unless $m {
        die "The input is not a valid INI file.";
    }
```

```
    return $m.made
}

say parse-ini($ini).perl;

use Test;

is-deeply parse-ini("k = v\n", :rule<pair>), 'k' => 'v',
    'can parse a simple pair';
done-testing;
```

To better encapsulate all the parsing functionality within the grammar, we can turn parse-ini into a method:

```
grammar IniFile {
    # regexes/tokens unchanged as before

    method parse-ini(Str $input, :$rule = 'TOP') {
        my $m = self.parse($input,
            :actions(IniFile::Actions),
            :$rule,
        );
        unless $m {
            die "The input is not a valid INI file.";
        }

        return $m.made
    }
}

# Usage:

my $result = IniFile.parse-ini($text);
```

To make this work, the class IniFile::Actions either has to be declared before the grammar, or needs to be predeclared with class IniFile::Action { ... } at the top of the file (with the literal three dots to mark it as a forward declaration).

9.7 Generating Good Error Messages

Good error messages are paramount to the user experience of any product. Parsers are no exception to this. Consider the difference between the message Square bracket [on line 3 closed by curly bracket } on line 5, in contrast to Python's lazy and generic SyntaxError: invalid syntax.

In addition to the textual message, knowing the location of the parse error helps tremendously in figuring out what's wrong.

We'll explore how to generate better parsing error messages from a grammar, using our INI file parser as an example.

9.7.1 Failure Is Normal

Before we start, it's important to realize that in a grammar-based parser, it's normal for a regex to fail to match, even in an overall successful parse.

Let's recall a part of the parser:

```
token block { [<pair> | <comment>]* }
token section { <header> <block> }
token TOP { <block> <section>* }
```

When this grammar matches against the string

```
key=value
[header]
other=stuff
```

then TOP calls block, which calls both pair and comment. The pair match succeeds; the comment match fails. No big deal. But since there is a * quantifier in token block, it tries again to match pair or comment. Neither succeeds, but the overall match of token block still succeeds.

A nice way to visualize passed and failed submatches is to install the Grammar::Tracer module (zef install Grammar::Tracer) and simply add the statement use Grammar::Tracer before the grammar definition. This produces debug output showing which rules matched and which didn't:

```
TOP
| block
| | pair
| | | key
| | | * MATCH "key"
| | | ws
| | | * MATCH ""
| | | ws
| | | * MATCH ""
| | | value
| | | * MATCH "value"
| | | ws
| | | * MATCH ""
| | | ws
| | | * MATCH ""
| | * MATCH "key=value\n"
| | pair
| | | key
| | | * FAIL
| | * FAIL
| | comment
| | * FAIL
| * MATCH "key=value\n"
| section
...
```

9.7.2 Detecting Harmful Failure

To produce good parsing error messages, you must distinguish between expected and unexpected parse failures. As explained in the preceding, a match failure of a single regex or token is not generally an indication of a malformed input. But you can identify points where you know that once the regex engine got this far, the rest of the match must succeed.

If you recall `pair`

```
rule pair { <key>  '='  <value> \n+ }
```

we know that if a key was parsed, we really expect the next character to be an equals sign. If not, the input is malformed.

In code, this is written like so:

```
rule pair {
    <key>
    [ '=' || <expect('=')> ]
    <value> \n+
}
```

`||` is a sequential alternative, which first tries to match the subregex on the left-hand side and only executes the right-hand side if that failed.

So now we have to define `expect`:

```
method expect($what) {
    die "Cannot parse input as INI file: Expected $what";
}
```

Yes, you can call methods just like regexes, because regexes really *are* methods under the hood. die throws an exception, so now the malformed input `justakey` produces the error

```
Cannot parse input as INI file: Expected =
```

followed by a backtrace. That's already better than "invalid syntax," though the position is still missing. Inside method `expect`, we can find the current parsing position through the method `pos`, which is supplied by the implicit parent class Grammar[9] that the `grammar` declaration brings with it.

We can use that to improve the error message a bit:

```
method expect($what) {
    die "Cannot parse input as INI file: Expected $what at
    character {self.pos}";
}
```

9.7.3 Providing Context

For larger inputs, we really want to print the line number. To calculate that, we need to get hold of the target string, which is available via the method `target`:

```
method expect($what) {
    my $parsed-so-far = self.target.substr(0, self.pos);
    my @lines = $parsed-so-far.lines;
    die "Cannot parse input as INI file: Expected $what at line
    @lines.elems(), after '@lines[*-1]'";
}
```

This brings us from the "meh" realm of error messages to quite good. Thus

```
IniFile.parse(q:to/EOI/);
key=value
[section]
key_without_value
more=key
EOI
```

---

[9]https://docs.raku.org/type/Grammar

now dies with

```
Cannot parse input as INI file: Expected = at line 3, after
'key_without_value'
```

You can further refine the expect method by providing context both before and after the position of the parse failure. And of course you have to apply the [thing || <expect('thing')>] pattern at more places inside the regex to get better error messages.

Finally, you can provide different kinds of error messages too. For example, when parsing a section header, once the initial [is parsed, you likely don't want an error message "expected rest of section header" but rather "malformed section header, at line …":

```
rule pair {
    <key>
    [ '=' || <expect('=')> ]
    [ <value> || <expect('value')>]
    \n+
}
token header {
    '['
    [ ( <-[ \[ \] \n ]>+ )    ']'
        || <error("malformed section header")> ]
    \n+
}
...

method expect($what) {
    self.error("expected $what");
}

method error($msg) {
    my $parsed-so-far = self.target.substr(0, self.pos);
```

```
    my @lines = $parsed-so-far.lines;
    die "Cannot parse input as INI file: $msg at line @lines.
    elems(), after '@lines[*-1]'";
}
```

Since Rakudo uses grammars to parse Raku input, you can use Rakudo's own grammar[10] as a source of inspiration for more ways to make error reporting even better.

9.7.4 Shortcuts for Parsing Matching Pairs

Since it's such a common task, Raku grammars have a special *goal-matching* syntax for matching a pair of delimiters with something between them. In the INI file example, that's a pair of brackets with a section header between them.

We can change

```
token header { '[' ( <-[ \[ \] \n ]>+ ) ']' \n+ }
```

to read

```
token header { '[' ~ ']' ( <-[ \[ \] \n ]>+ ) \n+ }
```

Not only does this have the aesthetic benefit of putting the matching delimiters closer together; it also calls a method FAILGOAL for us if everything except the closing delimiter matched. We can use this to generate better error messages for parse failures of matched pairs:

```
method FAILGOAL($goal) {
    my $cleaned-goal = $goal.trim;
    $cleaned-goal = $0 if $goal ~~ / \' (.+) \' /;
    self.error("Cannot find closing $cleaned-goal");
}
```

---

[10]https://github.com/rakudo/rakudo/blob/nom/src/Perl6/Grammar.nqp

The argument passed to FAILGOAL is the string of the regex source code that failed to match the closing delimiter, here ']' (with a trailing space). From that we want to extract the literal] for the error message, hence the regex match in the middle of the method. If that regex matches successfully, the literal is in $/[0], for which $0 is a shortcut.

All parsing constructs using ~ can benefit from such a method FAILGOAL, so writing one is worth the effort in a grammar that parses several distinct quoting or bracketing constructs.

9.8 Write Your Own Grammars

Parsing is a skill that must be learned, mostly separately from your ordinary programming skills. So I encourage you to start with something small, like a parser for CSV or comma-separated values.[11] It's tempting to write a whole grammar for that in one go, but instead I recommend starting with parsing some atoms (like a cell of data between two commas), testing it, and only then proceeding to the next one.

And even in something as deceptively simple as CSV, some complexity lurks. For example, you could allow quoted strings that themselves can contain the separator character and an escape character that allows you to use the quoting character inside a quoted string.

For a deeper treatment of Raku regexes and grammars, check out *Parsing with Perl 6 Regexes and Grammars* by Moritz Lenz (Apress, 2017).

9.9 Summary

Raku allows regex reuse by treating them as first-class citizens, allowing them to be named and called like normal routines. Further clutter is removed by allowing whitespace inside regexes.

---

[11]https://en.wikipedia.org/wiki/Comma-separated_values

These features allow you to write regexes to parse proper file formats and even programming languages. Grammars let you structure, reuse, and encapsulate regexes.

The result of a regex match is a Match object, which is really a tree with nodes for each named submatch and for each capturing group. Action methods make it easy to decouple parsing from data extraction.

To generate good error messages from a parser, you need to distinguish between expected and unexpected match failures. The sequential alternative || is a tool you can use to turn unexpected match failures into error messages by raising an exception from the second branch of the alternative.

CHAPTER 10

A File and Directory Usage Graph

You bought a shiny new 8TB disk just a short while ago, and you're already getting low disk space warnings. What's taking up all that space?

To answer this question, and experiment a bit with data visualization, let's write a small tool that visualizes which files use up how much disk space. We also get to explore some functional programming concepts in the process.

10.1 Reading File Sizes

To visualize file usage, we must first recursively read all directories and files in a given directory and record their sizes. To get a listing of all elements in a directory, we can use the dir[1] function, which returns a lazy list of IO::Path[2] objects.

---

[1]https://docs.raku.org/routine/dir
[2]https://docs.raku.org/type/IO::Path

© Moritz Lenz 2020
M. Lenz, *Raku Fundamentals*, https://doi.org/10.1007/978-1-4842-6109-5_10

We distinguish between directories, which can have child entries, and files, which can't. Both can have a direct size and, in the case of directories also a total size, which includes files and subdirectories, recursively:

```
class File {
    has $.name;
    has $.size;
    method total-size() { $.size }
}

class Directory {
    has $.name;
    has $.size;
    has @.children;
    has $!total-size;
    method total-size() {
        $!total-size //= $.size + @.children.map({.total-
        size}).sum;
    }
}

sub tree(IO::Path $path) {
    if $path.d {
        return Directory.new(

            name     => $path.basename,
            size     => $path.s,
            children => dir($path).map(&tree),
        );
    }
    else {
```

```
    return File.new(
        name => $path.Str,
        size => $path.s,
    );
  }
}
```

The code for reading a file tree recursively uses the d and s methods on IO::Path. d returns True for directories and False for files. s returns the size.

Just to check that we've got a sensible data structure, we can write a short routine that prints it recursively, with indentation to indicate nesting of directory entries:

```
sub print-tree($tree, Int $indent = 0) {
    say ' ' x $indent, format-size($tree.total-size), ' ',
    $tree.name;
    if $tree ~~ Directory {
        print-tree($_, $indent + 2) for $tree.children
    }
}

sub format-size(Int $bytes) {
    my @units = flat '', <k M G T P>;
    my @steps = (1, { $_ * 1024 } ... *).head(6);
    for @steps.kv -> $idx, $step {
        my $in-unit = $bytes / $step;
        if $in-unit < 1024 {
            return sprintf '%.1f%s', $in-unit, @units[$idx];
        }
    }
}
```

```
sub MAIN($dir = '.') {
    print-tree(tree($dir.IO));
}
```

The subroutine `print-tree` is pretty boring, if you're used to recursion. It prints out the name and size of the current node and, if the current node is a directory, recurses into each child with an increased indentation. The indentation is applied through the x string repetition operator, which when called as `$string x $count` repeats the `$string` `$count` times. It uses the `~~` smart matching operator to perform a type check; it tests if `$tree` is a `Directory`.

To get a human-readable representation of the size of a number, `format-size` knows a list of six units: the empty string for one, k (kilo) for 1024, M (mega) for 1024×1024, and so on. This list is stored in the array `@units`. The multiple associated with each unit is stored in `@steps`, which is initialized through the *series* operator …. Its structure is `INITIAL,` `CALLABLE ... LIMIT`, where it applies `CALLABLE` first to the initial value and then to the next value generated and so on, until it hits `LIMIT`. The limit here is *, a special term called *Whatever*, which means it's unlimited. Thus, the sequence operator returns a lazy, potentially infinite, list, and the trailing `.head(6)` call limits it to six values.

To find the most appropriate unit to print with the size, we have to iterate over both the values and the indices of the array, which `for @steps.kv -> $idx, $step { .. }` accomplishes. `sprintf`, known from other programming languages, does the actual formatting to one digit after the dot and appends the unit.

10.2 Generating a Tree-Map

One possible visualization of file and directory sizes is a *tree-map*, which represents each directory as a rectangle and each file inside it as a rectangle within the directory's rectangle. The size of each rectangle is proportional to the size of the file or directory it represents.

We'll generate an SVG file containing all those rectangles. Modern browsers support displaying such files and also show mouse-over texts for each rectangle. This alleviates the burden of actually labeling the rectangles, which can be quite a hassle.

To generate the SVG, we'll use the SVG module, which you can install with

```
$ zef install SVG
```

This module provides a single static method, into which you pass nested pairs. Pairs whose values are arrays are turned into XML tags; other pairs are turned into attributes. As an example, this script

```
use SVG;
print SVG.serialize(
    :svg[
        width => 100,
        height => 20,
        title => [
            'example',
        ]
    ],
);
```

produces this output:

```
<svg xmlns="http://www.w3.org/2000/svg"
    xmlns:svg="http://www.w3.org/2000/svg"
    xmlns:xlink="http://www.w3.org/1999/xlink"
    width="100"
    height="20">
        <title>example</title>
</svg>
```

(without the indentation). The xmlns-tags are helpfully added by the SVG module and are necessary for programs to recognize the file as SVG.

Returning to the tree-maps (Figure 10-1), a very simple way to lay out
the rectangle is to recurse into areas, and for each area subdivide it either
horizontally or vertically, depending upon which axis is longer:

```
sub tree-map($tree, :$x1!, :$x2!, :$y1!, :$y2) {
    # do not produce rectangles for small files/dirs
    return if ($x2 - $x1) * ($y2 - $y1) < 20;

    # produce a rectangle for the current file or dir
    take 'rect' => [
        x       => $x1,
        y       => $y1,
        width   => $x2 - $x1,
        height  => $y2 - $y1,
        style   => "fill:" ~ random-color(),
        title   => [$tree.name],
    ];
    return if $tree ~~ File;

    if $x2 - $x1 > $y2 - $y1 {
        # split along the x-axis
        my $base = ($x2 - $x1) / $tree.total-size;
        my $new-x = $x1;
        for $tree.children -> $child {
            my $increment = $base * $child.total-size;
            tree-map(
                $child,
                x1 => $new-x,
                x2 => $new-x + $increment,
                :$y1,
                :$y2,
            );
```

```raku
            $new-x += $increment;
        }
    }
    else {

        # split along the y-axis
        my $base = ($y2 - $y1) / $tree.total-size;
        my $new-y = $y1;
        for $tree.children -> $child {
            my $increment = $base * $child.total-size;
            tree-map(
                $child,
                :$x1,
                :$x2,
                y1 => $new-y,
                y2 => $new-y + $increment,
            );
            $new-y += $increment;
        }
    }
}

sub random-color {
    return 'rgb(' ~ (1..3).map({ (^256).pick }).join(',') ~ ')';
}

sub MAIN($dir = '.') {
    my $tree = tree($dir.IO);
    use SVG;
    my $width = 1024;
    my $height = 768;
    say SVG.serialize(
```

```
    :svg[
        :$width,
        :$height,
        | gather tree-map $tree, x1 => 0, x2 => $width,
        y1 => 0, y2 => $height
    ]
  );
}
```

Figure 10-1. *Tree-map of an example directory, with a mouse-over hover identifying one of the files*

The generated file is not pretty, due to the random colors and due to some files being identified as very narrow rectangles. But it does make it obvious that there are a few big files and many mostly small files in a directory (which happens to be the `.git` directory of a repository). Viewing a file in a browser shows the name of the file on the mouse-over.

How did we generate this file?

Sub `tree-map` calls `take` to add elements to a result list, so it must be called in the context of a `gather` statement. `gather { take 1; take 2 }` returns a lazy list of two elements, `1` and `2`. But the `take` calls don't have to occur in the lexical scope of the `gather`; they can be in any code that's directly or indirectly called from the `gather`. We call that the *dynamic scope*.

The rest of sub `tree-map` is mostly straightforward. For each direction in which the remaining rectangle can be split, we calculate a base unit that signifies how many pixels a byte should occupy. This is used to split up the current canvas into smaller ones and use those to recurse into `tree-map`.

The random color generation uses `^256` to create a range from 0 to 256 (exclusive), and `.pick` returns a random element from this range. The result is a random CSS color string like `rgb(120,240,5)`.

In sub MAIN, the `gather` returns a list, which would normally be nested inside the outer array. The pipe symbol `|` in `:svg[ ..., | gather ... ]` before the `gather` prevents the normal nesting and flattens the list into the outer array.

10.3 Flame Graphs

The disadvantage of tree-maps as generated in the preceding is that the human brain isn't very good at comparing the sizes of rectangles with different aspect ratios, especially if their widths are very different from their heights (i.e., very tall or very flat rectangles). Flame graphs prevent this perception error by showing file sizes as horizontal bars. The vertical arrangement indicates the nesting of directories and files inside other directories. The disadvantage is that less of the available space is used for visualizing the file sizes.

It is easier to generate flame graphs than tree-maps, because you only need to subdivide in one direction, whereas the height of each bar is fixed. Here it is set to 15 pixels:

```
sub flame-graph($tree, :$x1!, :$x2!, :$y!, :$height!) {
    return if $y >= $height;
    take 'rect' => [
        x       => $x1,
        y       => $y,
        width   => $x2 - $x1,
        height  => 15,
        style   => "fill:" ~ random-color(),
        title   => [$tree.name ~ ', ' ~ format-size($tree.total-
        size)],
    ];
    return if $tree ~~ File;

    my $base = ($x2 - $x1) / $tree.total-size;
    my $new-x = $x1;

    for $tree.children -> $child {
        my $increment = $base * $child.total-size;
        flame-graph(
            $child,
            x1 => $new-x,
            x2 => $new-x + $increment,
            y => $y + 15,
            :$height,
        );
        $new-x += $increment;
    }
}
```

We can add a switch to sub MAIN to call either tree-map or flame-graph, depending on a command-line option:

```
sub MAIN($dir = '.', :$type="flame") {
    my $tree = tree($dir.IO);
    use SVG;
    my $width = 1024;
    my $height = 768;
    my &grapher = $type eq 'flame'
            ?? { flame-graph $tree, x1 => 0, x2 => $width,
            y => 0, :$height }
            !! { tree-map    $tree, x1 => 0, x2 => $width,
            y1 => 0, y2 => $height }
    say SVG.serialize(
        :svg[
            :$width,
            :$height,
            | gather grapher()
        ]
    );
}
```

Since SVG's coordinate system places the zero of the vertical axis at the top, this actually produces an inverted flame graph, sometimes called an icicle graph (Figure 10-2):

Figure 10-2. *Inverted flame graph, where the width of each bar represents a file/directory size and the vertical position the nesting inside a directory*

This graph was generated by calling `dirstat --type=flame src/raku-fundamentals/`.

10.4 Functional Refactorings

There's a pattern that occurs three times in the code for generating tree-maps and flame graphs: dividing an area based on the size of the files and directories in the tree associated with the area.

Extracting such common code into a function is a good idea, but it's slightly hindered by the fact that there is custom code inside the loop that's part of the common code. Functional programming offers a solution: put the custom code inside a separate function, and have the common code call it.

Applying this technique to the tree graph flame graph looks like this:

```
sub subdivide($tree, $lower, $upper, &todo) {
    my $base = ($upper - $lower ) / $tree.total-size;
    my $var  = $lower;
    for $tree.children -> $child {
        my $incremented = $var + $base * $child.total-size;
        todo($child, $var, $incremented);
        $var = $incremented,
    }
}

sub flame-graph($tree, :$x1!, :$x2!, :$y!, :$height!) {
    return if $y >= $height;
    take 'rect' => [
        x       => $x1,
        y       => $y,
```

```
            width  => $x2 - $x1,
            height => 15,
            style  => "fill:" ~ random-color(),
            title  => [$tree.name ~ ', ' ~ format-size($tree.total-
            size)],
        ];
    return if $tree ~~ File;
    subdivide( $tree, $x1, $x2, -> $child, $x1, $x2 {
        flame-graph( $child, :$x1, :$x2, :y($y + 15), :$height );
    });
}

sub tree-map($tree, :$x1!, :$x2!, :$y1!, :$y2) {
    return if ($x2 - $x1) * ($y2 - $y1) < 20;
    take 'rect' => [
        x       => $x1,
        y       => $y1,
        width   => $x2 - $x1,
        height  => $y2 - $y1,
        style   => "fill:" ~ random-color(),
        title   => [$tree.name],
    ];
    return if $tree ~~ File;

    if $x2 - $x1 > $y2 - $y1 {
        # split along the x-axis
        subdivide $tree, $x1, $x2, -> $child, $x1, $x2 {
            tree-map $child, :$x1, :$x2, :$y1, :$y2;
        }
    }
```

```
else {
    # split along the y-axis
    subdivide $tree, $y1, $y2, -> $child, $y1, $y2 {
        tree-map $child, :$x1, :$x2, :$y1, :$y2;
    }
}
}
```

The newly introduced subroutine subdivide takes a directory tree, a start and end point, and finally a code object &todo. For each child of the directory tree, it calculates the new coordinates and then calls the &todo function.

The usage in subroutine flame-graph looks like this:

```
subdivide( $tree, $x1, $x2, -> $child, $x1, $x2 {
    flame-graph( $child, :$x1, :$x2, :y($y + 15), :$height );
});
```

The code object being passed to subdivide starts with ->, which introduces the signature of a block. The code block recurses into flame-graph, adding some extra arguments and turning two positional arguments into named arguments along the way.

This refactoring shortened the code and made it overall more pleasant to work with. But there's still quite a bit of duplication between tree-map and flame-graph: both have an initial termination condition, a take of a rectangle, and then a call or two to subdivide. If we're willing to put all the small differences into small, separate functions, we can unify it further.

If we were to pass all those new functions as arguments to each call, we would create an unpleasantly long argument list. Instead, we can use those functions to generate the previous functions flame-graph and tree-map:

```
sub svg-tree-gen(:&terminate!, :&base-height!, :&subdivide-x!,
:&other!) {
    sub inner($tree, :$x1!, :$x2!, :$y1!, :$y2!) {
        return if terminate(:$x1, :$x2, :$y1, :$y2);
```

```
    take 'rect' => [
        x       => $x1,
        y       => $y1,
        width => $x2 - $x1,
        height => base-height(:$y1, :$y2),
        style => "fill:" ~ random-color(),
        title => [$tree.name ~ ', ' ~ format-size($tree.
        total-size)],
    ];
    return if $tree ~~ File;
    if subdivide-x(:$x1, :$y1, :$x2, :$y2) {
        # split along the x-axis
        subdivide $tree, $x1, $x2, -> $child, $x1, $x2 {
            inner($child, :$x1, :$x2, :y1(other($y1)),
            :$y2);
        }
    }
    else {
        # split along the y-axis
        subdivide $tree, $y1, $y2, -> $child, $y1, $y2 {
            inner($child, :x1(other($x1)), :$x2, :$y1, :$y2);
        }
    }
}
}

my &flame-graph = svg-tree-gen
    terminate   => -> :$y1, :$y2, | { $y1 > $y2 },
    base-height => -> | { 15 },
    subdivide-x => -> | { True },
    other       => -> $y1 { $y1 + 15 },
    ;
```

```
my &tree-map = svg-tree-gen
    terminate   => -> :$x1, :$y1, :$x2, :$y2 { ($x2 - $x1) *
    ($y2 - $y1) < 20 },
    base-height => -> :$y1, :$y2 { $y2 - $y1 },
    subdivide-x => -> :$x1, :$x2, :$y1, :$y2 { $x2 - $x1 >
    $y2 - $y1 },
    other       => -> $a { $a },
    ;
```

Now we have a new function svg-tree-gen, which returns a function. The behavior of the returned function depends on the four small functions that svg-tree-gen receives as arguments.

The first argument, terminate, determines under what condition the inner function should terminate early. For tree-map, that's when the area is below 20 pixels; for flame-graph, that's when the current y-coordinate $y1 exceeds the height of the whole image (stored in $y2). svg-tree-gen always calls this function with the four named arguments x1, x2, y1, and y2, so the terminate function must ignore the x1 and x2 values. It does this by adding | as a parameter, which is an anonymous capture. Such a parameter can bind arbitrary positional and named arguments, and since it's an anonymous parameter, it discards all the values.

The second configuration function, base-height, determines the height of the rectangle in the base case. For flame-graph it's a constant, so the configuration function must discard all arguments, again with a |. For tree-graph, it must return the difference between $y2 and $y1, as before the refactoring.

The third function determines when to subdivide along the x axis. Flame graphs always divide along the x axis, so -> | { True } accomplishes that. Our simplistic approach to tree graphs divides along the longer axis, so only along the x axis if $x2 - $x1 > $y2 - $y1.

The fourth and final function we pass to svg-tree-gen calculates the coordinate of the axis that isn't being subdivided. In the case of flame-graph that's increasing over the previous value by the height of the bars, and for tree-map it's the unchanged coordinate, so we pass the identity function -> $a { $a }.

The inner function only needs a name because we need to call it from itself recursively; otherwise an anonymous function sub ($tree, :$x1!, :$x2!, :$y1!, :$y2!) { ... } would have worked fine.

This refactoring also unifies the names of the arguments to flame-graph and tree-map (previously, tree-map had :$y2 and flame-graph had :$height), so the call can now be simplified to

```
my &grapher = $type eq 'flame' ?? &flame-graph !! &tree-map;
say SVG.serialize(
    :svg[
        :$width,
        :$height,
        | do gather grapher $tree, x1 => 0, x2 => $width,
        y1 => 0, y2 => $height
    ]
);
```

Now that we have very compact definitions of flame-graph and tree-map, it's a good time to play with some of the parameters. Let's introduce a bit of margin in the flame graph by having the increment in other greater than the bar height in base-height:

```
my &flame-graph = svg-tree-gen
    base-height => -> | { 15 },
    other       => -> $y1 { $y1 + 16 },
    # rest as before
```

Another knob to turn is to change the color generation to something more deterministic and make it configurable from the outside:

```
sub svg-tree-gen(:&color=&random-color, :&terminate!, :&base-height!,
                 :&subdivide-x!, :&other!) {
   sub inner($tree, :$x1!, :$x2!, :$y1!, :$y2!) {
       return if terminate(:$x1, :$x2, :$y1, :$y2);
       take 'rect' => [
           x       => $x1,
           y       => $y1,
           width   => $x2 - $x1,
           height  => base-height(:$y1, :$y2),
           style   => "fill:" ~ color(),
           title   => [$tree.name ~ ', ' ~ format-size($tree.
           total-size)],
       ];
       # rest as before
}
```

We can, for instance, keep state within the color generator and return a slightly different color during each iteration:

```
sub color-range(|) {
   state ($r, $g, $b) = (0, 240, 120);
   $r = ($r + 5) % 256;
   $g = ($g + 10) % 256;
   $b = ($b + 15) % 256;
   return "rgb($r,$g,$b)";
}
```

State variables keep their values between calls to the same subroutine, and their initialization runs only on the first call. Hence, this function slightly increases the lightness in each color channel for each invocation, except when it reaches 256, where the modulo operator % resets it back to a small value.

If we plug this into our functions by passing `color => &color-range` to the calls to `svg-tree-gen`, we get much less chaotic-looking output (Figures 10-3 and 10-4):

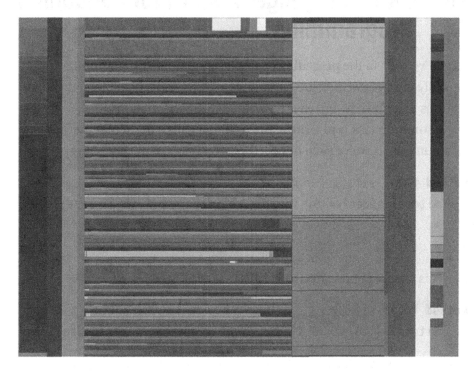

Figure 10-3. *Tree-map with deterministic color generation*

Figure 10-4. *Flame graph with deterministic color generation and one pixel margin between bars*

We could also pass in the coordinates to the &color routine, which would make it possible to write a color generator that produces a nice gradient.

10.5 More Language Support for Functional Programming

As you've seen in the preceding examples, functional programming typically involves writing lots of small functions. Raku has some language features that make it very easy to write such small functions.

A common task is to write a function that calls a particular method on its argument, as we've seen here:

```
method total-size() {
    $!total-size //= $.size + @.children.map({.total-size}).sum;
    #                                         ^^^^^^^^^^^^
}
```

This can be abbreviated to *.total-size:

```
method total-size() {
    $!total-size //= $.size + @.children.map(*.total-size).sum;
}
```

This works for chains of method calls too, so you could write @.children.map(*.total-size.round) if total-size returned a fractional number and you wanted to call the .round method on the result.

There are more cases where you can replace an expression with the "Whatever" star (*) to create a small function. To create a function that adds 15 to its argument, you can write * + 15 instead of -> $a { $a + 15 }.

If you need to write a function to just call another function, but pass more arguments to the second function, you can use the method assuming.[3] For example, `-> $x { f(42, $x }` can be replaced with `&f.assuming(42)`. This works also for named arguments, so `-> $x { f($x, height => 42 ) }` can be replaced with `&f.assuming(height => 42)`.

10.6 More Improvements

The classes `File` and `Directory` have some common functionality, like the `size` and the `name` attributes and the fact that they both have a method called `total-size`. A good way to factor out common behavior of classes is to put the common behavior into a *role*:

```
role Path {
    has $.name;
    has $.size;
    method total-size() { ... }
}

class File does Path {
    method total-size() { $.size }
}

class Directory does Path {
    has @.children;
    has $!total-size;
    method total-size() {
        $!total-size //= $.size + @.children.map(*.total-size).
        sum;
    }
}
```

---

[3]https://docs.raku.org/routine/assuming

A role looks structurally similar to a class, and using the does keyword in the class declaration applies the role to the class. This role application copies attributes and methods into the target class but with some additional compile-time checks. One such check is that a class must implement stubbed-out methods like method `total-size`, where the ... as the method body marked it as a stub. In addition, when you apply multiple roles to the same class, name clashes are detected and raise an error unless you implement the method in the class for disambiguation.

Roles are the preferred method of code reuse (apart from delegation) in Raku, because of the safety features mentioned previously.

Now that `File` and `Directory` have a common role, you can use that role as a type constraint for subroutines that expect one of these types, such as `sub subdivide(Path $tree, $lower, $upper, &todo)`.

Finally, the type argument to sub `MAIN` can have two possible values: `flame` for flame graphs or `tree` for tree-maps. A data structure that models this behavior is an *enum* or enumeration:

```
enum GraphType <flame tree>;

sub MAIN($dir = '.', GraphType :$type=flame) {
    my $tree = tree($dir.IO);

    use SVG;
    my $width = 1024;
    my $height = 768;
    my &grapher = $type == flame ?? &flame-graph !! &tree-map;
    say SVG.serialize(
        :svg[
            :$width,
```

```
        :$height,
        | do gather grapher $tree, x1 => 0, x2 => $width,
        y1 => 0, y2 => $height
    ]
);
}
```

The values of an enum are integers starting from zero, hence the comparison with == instead of eq. You can access the possible values of an enum either as short identifiers (flame) or through the namespace of the enum type, GraphType::flame.

Now if you obtain a help message from the script (by running it with the --help option), the type argument is automatically documented: --type=<GraphType> (flame tree).

10.7 Explore!

To get familiar with the functional programming concept, I encourage you to look through the code you've written so far and refactor near-duplicate code blocks into a common base and to swap out the code that differs into callbacks.

More importantly, try to find abstractions that make sense. In the visualization examples, the underlying principle is *divide and conquer.*[4] Can you come up with a general divide-and-conquer implementation that is still useful?

Thinking back to the tree-map and flame graphs, maybe you can separate the logic for sizing rectangles from the logic for placing the rectangles?

---

[4]https://en.wikipedia.org/wiki/Divide_and_conquer_algorithm

10.8 Summary

Functional programming offers techniques for extracting common logic into separate functions. The desired differences in behavior can be encoded in more functions that you pass in as arguments to other functions.

Raku supports functional programming by making functions first class, so you can pass them around as ordinary objects. It also offers closures (access to outer lexical variables from functions) and various shortcuts that make it more pleasant to write short functions.

CHAPTER 11

A Unicode Search Tool

Every so often, I have to identify or research some Unicode characters. There's a tool called uni[1] in the Perl 5 distribution App::Uni,[2] developed by Audrey Tang and Ricardo Signes.

Let's reimplement its basic functionality in a few lines of Raku code and use that as an occasion to talk about Unicode support in Raku

If you give it one character on the command line, it prints out a description of the following character:

```
$ uni њ
њ - U+0045a - CYRILLIC SMALL LETTER NJE
```

If you give it a longer string instead, it searches in the list of Unicode character names and prints out the same information for each character whose description matches the search string:

```
$ uni third|head -n3
⅓ - U+02153 - VULGAR FRACTION ONE THIRD
⅔ - U+02154 - VULGAR FRACTION TWO THIRDS
0/3 - U+02189 - VULGAR FRACTION ZERO THIRDS
```

---

[1]https://metacpan.org/pod/uni
[2]https://metacpan.org/release/App-Uni

© Moritz Lenz 2020
M. Lenz, *Raku Fundamentals*, https://doi.org/10.1007/978-1-4842-6109-5_11

Each line corresponds to what Unicode calls a "code point," which is usually a character on its own but occasionally also something like U+00300-COMBINING GRAVE ACCENT, which, combined with a-U+00061-LATIN SMALL LETTER A, makes the character à.

Raku offers a method uniname in both the classes Str and Int that produce the Unicode code point name for a given character, either in its direct character form or in the form of its code point number. With that, the first part of uni's desired functionality looks like this:

```
#!/usr/bin/env raku

use v6;

sub format-codepoint(Int $codepoint) {
    sprintf "%s - U+%05x - %s\n",
        $codepoint.chr,
        $codepoint,
        $codepoint.uniname;
}

multi sub MAIN(Str $x where .chars == 1) {
    print format-codepoint($x.ord);
}
```

Let's look at it in action:

```
$ uni ø
ø - U+000f8 - LATIN SMALL LETTER O WITH STROKE
```

The chr method turns a code point number into the character, and ord is the reverse: in other words, from character to code point number.

The second part, searching in all Unicode character names, works by brute force enumerating all possible characters and searching through their uniname:

```
multi sub MAIN($search is copy) {
    $search.=uc;
    for 1..0x10FFFF -> $codepoint {
        if $codepoint.uniname.contains($search) {
            print format-codepoint($codepoint);
        }
    }
}
```

Since all character names are in uppercase, the search term is first converted to uppercase with $search.=uc, which is short for $search = $search.uc. By default, parameters are read-only, which is why its declaration here uses its copy to prevent that.

Instead of this rather imperative style, we can also formulate it in a more functional style. We could think of it as a list of all characters, which we whittle down to those characters that interest us, to finally format them the way we want:

```
multi sub MAIN($search is copy) {
    $search.=uc;
    print (1..0x10FFFF).grep(*.uniname.contains($search))
                      .map(&format-codepoint)
                      .join;
}
```

To make it easier to identify (rather than search for) a string of more than one character, an explicit option can help disambiguate:

```
multi sub MAIN($x, Bool :$identify!) {
    print $x.ords.map(&format-codepoint).join;
}
```

`Str.ords` returns the list of code points that make up the string. With this multi-candidate of sub `MAIN` in place, we can do something like

```
$ uni --identify øre
ø - U+000f8 - LATIN SMALL LETTER O WITH STROKE
r - U+00072 - LATIN SMALL LETTER R
e - U+00065 - LATIN SMALL LETTER E
```

11.1 Code Points, Grapheme Clusters, and Bytes

As alluded to in the preceding, not all code points are fully fledged characters on their own. Or put another way, some things that we visually identify as a single character are actually made up of several code points. Unicode calls such sequences of one base character and potentially several combining characters as a *grapheme cluster*.

Strings in Raku are based on these grapheme clusters. If you get a list of characters in a string with `$str.comb`, or extract a substring with `$str.substr(0, 4)`, match a regex against a string, determine the length, or do any other operation on a string, the unit is always the grapheme cluster. This best fits our intuitive understanding of what a character is and avoids accidentally tearing apart a logical character through a `substr`, `comb`, or similar operation:

```
my $s = "ø\c[COMBINING TILDE]";
say $s;         # Output: ø̃
say $s.chars;   # Output: 1
```

The Uni[3] type is akin to a string and represents a sequence of codepoints. It is useful in edge cases but doesn't support the same wealth of operations as Str.[4] The typical way to go from Str to a Uni value is to use one of the NFC, NFD, NFKC, or NFKD methods, which yield a Uni value in the normalization form of the same name.

Below the Uni level, you can also represent strings as bytes by choosing an encoding. If you want to get from the string to the byte level, call the encode[5] method:

```
my $bytes = 'Raku'.encode('UTF-8');    # utf8:0x<52 61 6B 75>
```

UTF-8 is the default encoding and also the one Raku assumes when reading source files. The result is something that does the Blob[6] role: you can access individual bytes with positional indexing, such as $bytes[0]. The decode method[7] helps you convert a Blob to a Str.

If you print out a Blob with say(), you get a string representation of the bytes in hexadecimal. Accessing individual bytes produces an integer and thus will typically be printed in decimal.

If you want to print out the raw bytes of a blob, you can use the write method of an I/O handle:

```
$*OUT.write('Raku'.encode('UTF-8'));
```

---

[3]https://docs.raku.org/type/Uni
[4]https://docs.raku.org/type/Str
[5]https://docs.raku.org/type/Str#method_encode
[6]https://docs.raku.org/type/Blob.html
[7]https://docs.raku.org/type/Blob.html#method_decode

11.2 Numbers

Number literals in Raku aren't limited to the Arabic digits we are so used to in the English-speaking part of the world. All Unicode code points that have the Decimal_Number (short Nd) property are allowed, so you can, for example, use Eastern Arabic numerals[8] or from many other scripts:

```
say ٤٢;            # 42
```

The same holds true for string-to-number conversions:

```
say "٤٢".Int;      # 42
```

For other numeric code points, you can use the unival method to obtain its numeric value:

```
say "\c[TIBETAN DIGIT HALF ZERO]".unival;
```

which produces the output -0.5 and also illustrates how to use a codepoint by name inside a string literal.

11.3 Other Unicode Properties

The uniprop method[9] in type Str returns the general category by default:

```
say "ø".uniprop;                            # Ll
say "\c[TIBETAN DIGIT HALF ZERO]".uniprop;  # No
```

The return value needs some Unicode knowledge in order to make sense of it, or one could read Unicode's Technical Report 44[10] for the gory details. Ll stands for Letter_Lowercase; No is Other_Number.

---

[8]https://en.wikipedia.org/wiki/Eastern_Arabic_numerals
[9]https://docs.raku.org/routine/uniprop
[10]http://unicode.org/reports/tr44/#Properties

This is what Unicode calls the *General Category*, but you can ask the uniprop (or uniprop-bool method if you're only interested in a boolean result) for other properties as well:

```
say "a".uniprop-bool('ASCII_Hex_Digit');    # True
say "ü".uniprop-bool('Numeric_Type');        # False
say ".".uniprop("Word_Break");               # MidNumLet
```

11.4 Collation

Sorting strings starts to become complicated when you're not limited to ASCII characters. Raku's sort method uses the cmp infix operator, which does a pretty standard lexicographic comparison based on the codepoint number.

If you need to use a more sophisticated collation algorithm, Rakudo 2017.09 and newer offer the Unicode Collation Algorithm[11] through the collate method:

```
my @list = <a ö ä Ä o ø>;
say @list.sort;                      # (a o Ä ä ö ø)

say @list.collate;                   # (a ä Ä o ö ø)
$*COLLATION.set(:tertiary(False));
say @list.collate;                   # (a Ä ä o ö ø)
```

The default sort considers any character with diacritics to be larger than ASCII characters, because that's how they appear in the code point list. On the other hand, collate knows that characters with diacritics belong directly after their base character, which is not perfect in every language[12] but usually a good compromise.

---

[11]http://unicode.org/reports/tr10/
[12]For example, Norwegian sorts å after z, not after a.

For Latin-based scripts, the primary sorting criterion is alphabetical, the secondary is diacritics, and the third is case. `$*COLLATION.set(:tertiary(False))` thus makes `.collate` ignore case, so it doesn't force lowercase characters to come before uppercase characters anymore.

At the time of writing, language-specific collation has not yet been implemented in Raku.

11.5 Summary

Raku takes languages other than English very seriously and goes to great lengths to facilitate working with them and the characters they use.

This includes basing strings on grapheme clusters rather than code points, support for non-Arabic digits in numbers, and access to large parts of the Unicode database through built-in methods.

CHAPTER 12

Creating a Web Service and Declarative APIs

Nowadays, it seems like every software must be reachable through the network, in the cloud.

In this spirit, we'll take a look at a simple way to create a web service in Raku by using Cro,[1] a set of libraries that makes it easy to write asynchronous web clients and services. The name Cro comes from a terrible pun: it allows me to write microservices, my *cro* services.

Later in this chapter, we'll take a look at how Cro achieves its declarative API.

12.1 Getting Started with Cro

We'll reuse the code from Chapter 4, which converts UNIX timestamps into ISO-formatted datetime strings and vice versa, and now expose them through HTTP.

---

[1]https://cro.services/

© Moritz Lenz 2020
M. Lenz, *Raku Fundamentals*, https://doi.org/10.1007/978-1-4842-6109-5_12

The first part, converting from UNIX timestamp to ISO date, goes like this[2]:

```
use Cro::HTTP::Router;
use Cro::HTTP::Server;

my $application = route {
    get -> 'datetime', Int $timestamp {
        my $dt = DateTime.new($timestamp);
        content 'text/plain', "$dt\n";
    }
}
my $port = 8080;
my Cro::Service $service = Cro::HTTP::Server.new(
    :host<0.0.0.0>,
    :$port,
    :$application,
);

$service.start;
say "Application started on port $port";
react whenever signal(SIGINT) { $service.stop; done; }
```

In this example, we see the subroutines route, get, and content that are exported by the modules Cro::HTTP::Router.

route takes a block as an argument and returns an application. Inside the block, we can call get (or other HTTP verb functions such as post or put) to declare *routes*, pieces of code that Cro calls for us when somebody requests the matching URL through HTTP.

Here, the route declaration starts as get -> 'datetime', Int $timestamp. The -> arrow introduces a signature, and Cro interprets each argument as a part of a slash-delimited URL. In our example, the URL

---

[2]Read on for instructions on how to install Cro.

that matches the signature is /datetime/ followed by an integer, like /
datetime/1578135634. When Cro receives such a request, it uses the
constant string datetime to identify the route and puts the 1578135634 into
the variable $timestamp.

The logic for converting the timestamp to a DateTime object is familiar
from Chapter 4; the only difference is that instead of using say to print the
result to standard output, we use the content function to serve the back to
the HTTP requester. This is necessary because each HTTP response needs
to declare its content type so that, for example, a browser knows whether
to render the response as HTML, as an image, etc. The text/plain content
type denotes, as the name says, plain text that is not to be interpreted in
any special way.

The code after is classical plumbing: it instantiates a
Cro::HTTP::Server object at a given TCP port (here 8080; feel free to
change it to your liking) and our collection of one meager route and
then tells it to start serving HTTP requests. We chose the host 0.0.0.0
(which means bind to all IP addresses) so that if you run the application
in a Docker container, it can be reached from the host. If you do not use
Docker, using 127.0.0.1 or localhost is safer, as it doesn't expose the
application to other machines in the network.

Then finally, the shocker line:

```
react whenever signal(SIGINT) { $service.stop; done; }
```

The signal() function returns a Supply,[3] which is an asynchronous
data stream, hereof inter-process communication signals. signal(SIGINT)
specifically only emits events when the process receives the INT or
interrupt signal, which you can typically create by pressing the keys Ctrl+C
in your terminal.

---

[3]https://docs.raku.org/language/concurrency#Supplies

react is usually used in its block form, react { .... } and shortened here because it applies to only one statement. It runs and dispatches supplies in whenever statements until the code calls the done function (or all the streams finish, which doesn't happen for the signal streams).

So, inside react, whenever signal(SIGINT) { ... } calls the code marked by ..., each time the SIGINT signal is received – in which case we stop the HTTP server and exit the react construct.

If you want to handle other signals, such as SIGTERM (which is used by the kill system command), you can replace signal(SIGINT) by

```
signal(SIGINT).merge(signal(SIGTERM))
```

All of this is a complicated way to exit the program when somebody presses Ctrl+C.

Due to the asynchronous nature of Cro, you could also do other things here, like processing other supplies in the react block (like period timers, streams of file change events), while the HTTP server is merrily running.

To run this, first install the cro and Cro::HTTP::Test modules with the zef package manger:

```
$ zef install --/test cro Cro::HTTP::Test
```

where the --/test option tells zef not to run the module tests, which both take a long time, and require some local infrastructure that you are unlikely to have available.

If you use Docker to run your raku programs, you can use the image moritzlenz/raku-fundamentals, which builds on Rakudo Star and includes the necessary cro modules. If you go that route, you must also use docker's --expose command-line option to make the service available on the host; otherwise, it's only reachable from within the container. Then the command line looks like this:

```
$ docker run --rm --publish 8080:8080 -v $PW/raku -w /raku \
    -it moritzlenz/raku-fundamentals raku datetime.p6
```

We can test the service on the command line with an HTTP client like curl[4]:

```
$ curl http://127.0.0.1:8080/datetime/1578135634
2020-01-04T11:00:34Z
```

12.2 Expanding the Service

Now that we have a minimalistic but working service, we can incorporate the conversion from an ISO datetime string to a UNIX timestamp. We'll just be looking at the route block; everything stays the same. Here's one approach to implement it:

```
my token date-re {
    ^
    \d**4 '-' \d**2 '-' \d** 2 # date part YYYY-MM-DD
    [
    ' '
    \d**2 ':' \d**2 ':' \d**2 # time
    ]?
    $
}

my $application = route {
    get -> 'datetime', Int $timestamp {
        my $dt = DateTime.new($timestamp);
        content 'text/plain', "$dt\n";
    }
    get -> 'datetime', Str $date_spec where &date-re {
        my ( $date_str, $time_str ) = $date_spec.split(' ');
        my $date = Date.new($date_str);
```

---

[4]https://curl.haxx.se/

```
    my $datetime;
    if $time_str {
        my ( $hour, $minute, $second ) = $time_str.
        split(':');
        $datetime = DateTime.new( :$date, :$hour, :$minute,
        :$second );
    }
    else {
        $datetime = $date.DateTime;
    }
    content "text/plain", $datetime.posix ~ "\n";
  }
}
```

We start with a regex that defines how the datetime format that we want to accept looks like and store it in the variable &date-re. Then in the route { ... } block, we add a second get call with this signature:

```
get -> 'datetime', Str $date_spec where &date-re { ... }
```

This defines a second route, under a similar url as before, /datetime/ YYYY-MM-DD HH:MM:SS (where the time part is optional). The logic is again copied from Chapter 4, so no surprises here. The only difference is that with the command-line application, the command-line parser split the date and time part for us, which we now explicitly do with a call to .split(' ').

When we test this code with curl or a browser, we need to remember that we cannot directly include a space in an URL directly but need to escape that as %20. After starting our extended service, we can call curl again to test it:

```
$ curl http://127.0.0.1:8080/datetime/2020-01-04%2011:00:34
1578135634
```

Most modern webservices tend to respond with JSON data, which we can achieve by passing a JSON-serializable data structure like a hash to the content function:

```
# in the first route
content 'application/json', {
    input => $timestamp,
    result => $dt.Str,
}

# in the second route
content "application/json", {
    input => $date_spec,
    result => $datetime.posix,
}
```

12.3 Testing

Testing a web application can be a bit of a pain sometimes. You have to start the application server, but first you need to find a free port where it can listen, and then you make your requests to the server, and tear it down afterward.

With a tiny bit of restructuring and the Cro::HTTP::Test module, all of this can be avoided.

For the restructuring, let's put our call to route into a subroutine of our own and put the server setup into a MAIN function:

```
sub routes() {
    return route {
        # same route definitions as before
    }
}
```

```raku
multi sub MAIN(Int :$port = 8080, :$host = '0.0.0.0') {
    my Cro::Service $service = Cro::HTTP::Server.new(
        :$host
        :$port,
        application => routes(),
    );

    $service.start;
    say "Application started on port $port";
    react whenever signal(SIGINT) { $service.stop; done; }
}
```

You can start the HTTP server as before, now with the added benefit of being able to override the port and the host (the IP that the server listens on) through the command line.

Our goal was testing, so let's add another MAIN multi for that.

```raku
multi sub MAIN('test') {
    use Cro::HTTP::Test;
    use Test;
    test-service routes(), {
        test get('/datetime/1578135634'),
            status => 200,
            json => {
                result => "2020-01-04T11:00:34Z",
                input => 1578135634 ,
            };
        test get('/datetime/2020-01-04%2011:00:34'),
            status => 200,
            json => {
                input => '2020-01-04 11:00:34',
                result => 1578135634,
            };
```

```
    }
    done-testing;
}
```

We meet our newest friend, sub test-service. We call it with two arguments, the routes to be tested and a block with our tests. Inside this block, the get() routine calls the appropriate routes without any server being started and returns an object of type Cro::HTTP::Test::TestRequest. With the test routine, we can check that this test response fulfills our expectations, here regarding the response code (status) and the JSON response body.

We can run the tests by adding the test command line parameter and get test output like this:

```
$ raku datetime.p6 test
    ok 1 - Status is acceptable
    ok 2 - Content type is recognized as a JSON one
    ok 3 - Body is acceptable
    1..3
ok 1 - GET /datetime/1578135634
    ok 1 - Status is acceptable
    ok 2 - Content type is recognized as a JSON one
    ok 3 - Body is acceptable
    1..3
ok 2 - GET /datetime/2020-01-04%2011:00:34
1..2
```

Each call to test produces one test in the output and a subtest (indicated by indentation) for each individual comparison.

12.4 Adding a Web Page

We have our mini web service at a place now where another program can talk to it comfortably through JSON over HTTP, but that's not really friendly toward end users.

As a demonstration for a possible user interface, let's add an HTML page that can be viewed in a browser. Since we'll handle the data through HTTP requests triggered from JavaScript, we can get away with serving static files. Cro offers a helper for that called static, which replaces our calls to content. Let's add these two routes to the route { ... } block:

```
get -> { static 'index.html'; }
get -> 'index.js' { static 'index.js'; }
```

The first one has an empty signature and so corresponds to the / (root) URL and serves the file index.html. The second one serves a file called index.js with the same URL.

The static helper can do more, like serving whole directories while preventing malicious path traversal,[5] but for our cases, the simple form is enough.

File index.html should be placed directly next to the raku script and can look like this:

```
<html>
  <head>
    <title>Datetime to UNIX timestamp conversion</title>
      <script
        src="https://code.jquery.com/jquery-3.5.1.min.js"
        crossorigin="anonymous"></script>
      <script type="text/javascript" src="/index.js"></script>
  </head>
```

---

[5]https://cro.services/docs/reference/cro-http-router#Serving_static_content

170

```html
<body>
  <h1>Convert UNIX timestamp to ISO datetime or vice
  versa</h1>
    <form>
      <label for="in">Input</label>
      <input name="in" id="in" placeholder="2014-01-14
      10:12:00"></input>
      <button id="submit">Submit</button>
    </form>
    <h2>Result</h2>
    <ul id="result"></ul>
</body>
</html>
```

The visible elements are just some headings, an input form and a
button for submitting it, as well as an empty list for the results.

We'll add some JavaScript in index.js to bring it to life:

```javascript
$(document).ready(function() {
    $('#submit').click(function(event) {
        var val = $('#in').val();
        $.get('/datetime/' + val, function(response) {
            $('#result').append(
                '<li>Input: ' + val +
                ', Result: ' + response['result'] +
                '</li>');
        });
        event.preventDefault();
    });
});
```

This piece of code uses the jQuery[6] library and subscribes to click events on the button. When the button is pressed, it reads the text from the input element, submits it asynchronously toward the URL /datetime/ followed by the input, and appends the result as list items to the unordered list (<ul>).

This is far from perfect, as the web application is missing error handling and visual appeal, but it does illustrate how you can have a pretty machine-focused API endpoint in your application and then put a user interface on top that uses HTML and javascript.

Convert UNIX timestamp to ISO datetime or vice versa

Input `1608850800` | Submit |

Result

- Input: 2020-10-20 11:22:33, Result: 1603192953
- Input: 1608850800, Result: 2020-12-24T23:00:00Z

Figure 12-1. *The minimalistic web frontend to the datetime conversion app*

There are several projects that aim to keep the JavaScript code composable and maintainable, like Vue.js,[7] angular,[8] and React.[9] In fact, the Cro documentation comes with a tutorial for building a single page application with React and Redux,[10] which you should follow if you want to dive deeper into this subject.

---

[6]https://jquery.com/
[7]https://vuejs.org/
[8]https://angular.io/
[9]https://reactjs.org/
[10]https://cro.services/docs/intro/spa-with-cro

12.5 Declarative APIs

We could now grow our application with more routes, authentication,[11] and more, but instead I want to draw attention to how Cro creates its APIs.

The syntax for routes looks like this:

```
get -> 'datetime', Int $timestamp { ... }
```

The get here is a function call, so we could also write this as

```
get(-> 'datetime', Int $timestamp { ... });
```

The arrow -> introduces a block with a signature. It's not really important that it's a block; an ordinary subroutine works as well:

```
get( sub ('datetime', Int $timestamp) { ... } )
```

In fact, there is no need to put the declaration of the subroutine inside the get call. We could have written instead:

```
sub convert-from-timestamp('datetime', Int $timestamp) {
    my $dt = DateTime.new($timestamp);
    content 'application/json', {
        input => $timestamp,
        result => $dt.Str,
    }
}
sub convert-from-isodate('datetime', Str $date_spec where
&date-re) {
    # omitted for brevity
}
```

---

[11]https://cro.services/docs/http-auth-and-sessions

```
my $application = route {
    get &convert-from-timestamp;
    get &convert-from-isodate;
}
```

get is a function that takes another function as an argument, something we've seen in Chapter 12. In contrast to those examples, get doesn't just call the function it receives; it *introspects* its signature to figure out when to call it.

We could do that too. In the context of the previous example, you could write

```
my @params = &convert-from-timestamp.signature.params;
say @params.elems;              # => 2
say @params[0].type;            # => (Str)
say @params[0].constraints;     # => all(datetime)
```

Through the .signature.params method chain, we obtain a list of Parameter[12] objects representing each function parameter; we can ask them for the type, additional constraints (like the string datetime used on the first parameter), the variable name, and many more properties.

Just like get, route { ... } is a function that calls its argument function after a bit of setup. It sets up a dynamic variable that get latches on to, which enables route to return an object with information about all the calls to get and so all the routes.

To illustrate this principle, let's try to write some functions that allow you to write small dispatchers based on the types, that is, call the first function with a matching type:

```
my &d = dispatcher {
    on -> Str $x { say "String $x" }
    on -> Date $x { say "Date $x" }
}
```

---

[12]https://docs.raku.org/type/Parameter

```
d(Date.new('2020-12-24'));
d("a test");
```

To make this aspirational example a valid Raku code, we need two
functions, dispatcher and on, that both take one callable block as an
argument. dispatcher needs to declare a dynamic variable and on
performs some sanity checks and adds its argument to the dynamic
variable:

```
sub dispatcher(&body) {
    my @*CASES;
    body();
    my @cases = @*CASES;
    return sub (Mu $x) {
        for @cases -> &case {
            if $x ~~ &case.signature.params[0].type {
                return case($x)
            }
        }
        die "No case matched $x";
    }
}

sub on(&case) {
    die "Called on() outside a dispatcher block"
        unless defined @*CASES;
    unless &case.signature.params == 1 {
        die "on() expects a block with exactly one parameter"
    }
    @*CASES.push: &case;
}
```

Sub `dispatcher` has to copy the contents of its dynamic variable into a lexical variable `my @cases`, because the dynamic variable is scoped to the execution time of the function it is declared in, so it ceases to exist after function `dispatcher` has returned. But `dispatcher` needs the contents to do its work, iterating through the cases and calling the first one that matches. It does this in an anonymous function that it returns so that the programmer can reuse the matcher in several code locations.

On your first read of code using Cro, you might have thought that the `route` and `get` construct looked like language extensions; instead, they turn out to be cleverly named functions that receive other functions as arguments. You can use the same techniques in your own libraries and frameworks to create interfaces that feel natural to the programmer that uses them.

12.6 Summary

With the Cro libraries, you can expose functionality pretty easily through HTTP. First you create some routes (code that is called by Cro when somebody requests the matching URL) in a `route { ... }` block and then pass the routes to the HTTP server. You start the server, and you're done.

Each route communicates its response by calling the `content` function, specifying both the content type and the response body; JSON serialization happens automatically for the appropriate content type.

A user interface can be created through static HTML and JavaScript, possibly with the help of JavaScript application frameworks.

We have also seen how Cro achieves a natural feel for its API by providing higher-order functions (functions that receive other functions as arguments) and perform introspection on the signatures of these functions.

CHAPTER 13

What's Next?

If you got this far reading this book, you likely have a solid grasp on the basics of Raku by now.

The examples and discussions have touched on a wide variety of topics. We started with what Raku is and how you can run Raku programs. Next up were the basic lexical structure of programs, variables, control flow, and I/O. The more advanced topics include object orientation, persistence, regexes and grammars, Unicode support, concurrency, and finally writing web services in Cro and designing intuitive programming interfaces.

But there's more to writing successful code than learning about the language. In this final chapter, I want to hint at some topics that you might want to pursue to help you keep your code base maintainable and to get it successfully in front of users.

13.1 Scaling Your Code Base

When your code base grows, it is often advisable to split it into separate files. You can create *modules* that contain your logic, organized by namespace and functionality. The scripts then tend to become shallow entry points that parse the command-line arguments, load the modules, and then call a function or method from a method to do the actual work.

In this scenario, tests are written as separate scripts, usually in a directory named t, that load and test the same modules.

© Moritz Lenz 2020
M. Lenz, *Raku Fundamentals*, https://doi.org/10.1007/978-1-4842-6109-5_13

The official documentation at `https://docs.raku.org/language/modules` explains how you can write modules, as well as the standard directory layout and metadata that the module installer `zef` (and other tooling) relies on.

As your code base grows, type annotations can help you to keep track of what arguments routines accept and what they return. I tend to use type annotations mostly in signatures that are part of a public API. With "public" I mean routines that can be accessed from outside the module they are in. Inside the routines, I tend to omit them for brevity and flexibility.

To make type constraints more reusable, you can define create subset types. For example, we've seen an example with an ad hoc–type constraint:

```
multi sub MAIN(Str $date where /^ \d+ \- \d+ \- \d+ $ /) { ...
}
```

Instead, you could create a subset type and use it several times:

```
subset DateStr of Str where /^ \d+ \- \d+ \- \d+ $ /;

multi sub MAIN(DateStr $date) { ... }
sub parse-date(DateStr) returns Date { ... }
```

You can collect several of these types in a module and import them wherever you need them.

13.2 Packaging Your Application

In order to deploy your application to users, you typically put it in some kind of self-contained archive or package.

Independent of the desired distribution format, the starting point is always the directory layout and metadata that the `zef` module installer uses, which is described at `https://docs.raku.org/language/modules`.

Raku packaging is still in active development, so instead of giving recipes, I want to briefly mention some options that you might find worth exploring.

13.2.1 Packaging As a Traditional Raku Module

Traditionally, Raku modules and software are distributed as tar archives[1] that contain the source code and some metadata, like a `META6.json` file.

Users need to have Rakudo and `zef` installed. They can then unpack the archive, go into the newly created directory, and install the software with `zef install`.

If your software is open source, you can add it to the official Raku ecosystem by uploading the package to PAUSE, the Perl Author's Upload Server. The official homepage at `https://pause.perl.org/pause/query` contains instructions on how to acquire an account, and the documentation at `https://docs.raku.org/language/modules#Upload_your_module_to_CPAN` contains instructions on how to create the tarball for upload.

An alternative is to keep the code on GitHub or GitLab and sending a pull request against the ecosystem git repository on GitHub.[2] In this pull request, you simply add a link to your `META6.json` file by editing the file `META.list` in said repository. The downside of this approach is that you cannot easily do release of your software and so users have a hard time obtaining a stable version.

Regardless of the approach, users can install your software through `zef` without having to download any package themselves.

---

[1]`www.gnu.org/software/tar/`
[2]`https://github.com/raku/ecosystem`

13.2.2 Deploying with Docker

Traditional Raku module distribution relies on a preinstalled Rakudo compiler, which might be a hassle for your users to install and a hassle for your to guide them to do it.

If you choose to distribute your application in a Docker image, you can base your image on the `rakudo-star` image and either use `zef install` or `COPY` instructions in your Dockerfile to install the application into a Docker image.

This is the most basic `Dockerfile` that builds on a preexisting image and installs that Raku application from the current working directory:

```
FROM rakudo-star:2020.1
COPY myapp /tmp/install
RUN zef install /tmp/install
ENTRYPOINT ["/usr/share/perl6/site/bin/myapp"]
```

Running `docker build -t myapp .` creates a Docker image `myapp`, which you can then distribute, with all dependencies included.

13.2.3 Windows Installers

The module App::InstallerMaker::WiX[3] can help you create a Windows `.msi` installer that creates a build of Rakudo, `zef`, and your application. It requires the Microsoft Visual C++ build tools and WiX.[4] You create a YAML file that describes your application and then run the script `make-perl6-wix-installer` to create a stand-alone `.msi` file.

---

[3]https://modules.raku.org/dist/App::InstallerMaker::WiX
[4]http://wixtoolset.org/releases/

13.3 Closing Thoughts

Raku is a big language, embedded in an even bigger community and ecosystem. A book such as this one cannot cover everything, but hopefully it helped you learn enough to perform most programming tasks in Raku and, more importantly, got you excited and motivated to explore and to learn more.

Index

A

Ansible's inventory files, 99

B

Backtracking, 109–111

C

Cron wrapper
  asynchronous interface, 60–63
  concurrent/parallel
      programs, 66–69
  extensions, 69
  higher-level primitives, 66
  mocking/testing, 72–78
  module installation, 79–80
  placing random points, 68
  random numbers, 68–69
  refactoring test, 70–72
  reliability/timing, 78–79
  run external commands, 60–63
  smart matching operator, 65
  STDOUT/STDERR
      streams, 61
  timeouts implementation, 64–66
  wrapped program, 59

Cro services
  authentication, 173–176
  command-line option, 164
  HTTP server, 164
  minimalistic web, 172
  parameter, 174
  signal() function, 163
  testing, 167–169
  UNIX timestamp, 161–162
  web page, 170–172

D, E

Datetime conversion
  automated tests, 46–51
  dealing time, 41
  debugging output, 33
  formatting, 36–38
  implicit variable/
      topic program, 42–44
  libraries, 32–33
  MAIN subs, 45
  numeric value, 33
  switch statement, 43
  timestamp, 38–41
  truncated-to method, 35
  UNIX timestamps, 31

© Moritz Lenz 2020
M. Lenz, *Raku Fundamentals*, https://doi.org/10.1007/978-1-4842-6109-5

Printed in the United States
By Bookmasters